Shhh! DON'T TALK ABOUT MENTAL HEALTH

WHY BEING QUIET IS NO LONGER AN OPTION

ARJUN GUPTA

Notion Press

Old No. 38, New No. 6
McNichols Road, Chetpet
Chennai - 600 031

First Published by Notion Press 2019
Copyright © Arjun Gupta 2019
All Rights Reserved.

ISBN 978-1-64546-971-1

This book has been published with all efforts taken to make the material error-free after the consent of the author. However, the author and the publisher do not assume and hereby disclaim any liability to any party for any loss, damage, or disruption caused by errors or omissions, whether such errors or omissions result from negligence, accident, or any other cause.

While every effort has been made to avoid any mistake or omission, this publication is being sold on the condition and understanding that neither the author nor the publishers or printers would be liable in any manner to any person by reason of any mistake or omission in this publication or for any action taken or omitted to be taken or advice rendered or accepted on the basis of this work. For any defect in printing or binding the publishers will be liable only to replace the defective copy by another copy of this work then available.

For my family.

My mom, my dad and my sisters.

I don't appreciate them enough.

Contents

Section III
Understanding Mental Illnesses

Contents

Contents

Contributors

Rajnandini Sarkar

Rajnandini Sarkar is an Applied Psychology student from Delhi University and a fashion blogger. She gets all her inspiration from YouTubers like Lilly Singh and Aakriti Rana who, in her own words, are 'complete boss ladies.' She works hard every day to be the best version of herself. She played a pivotal role in the making of this book as she assisted the author with research, literature review and presentation ideas. The book would be a lot less impressive without her.

Mental health is so important today. It is high time we talk about it, so I hope you enjoy reading a book that will empower you towards being your best version too.

– **Rajnandini Sarkar**

Rohit Kumar

Rohit Kumar, through his work and education, has come to believe that schools are places for an enriching socio-cultural dialogue. This can empower or subvert its pupils, depending upon how the school is imagined, designed and brought into action. Rohit holds an M.A. in Education from the Tata Institute of Social Sciences, Mumbai, India and a Master's in Software Systems from the Somaiya Institute of Management Studies and Research, Mumbai, India. However, he thinks his most important learning comes from two other experiences. One, working with youth from a variety of backgrounds to engage with their multicultural selves and Social Emotional Learning (SEL). And two, being a part of the summer staff team at the Seeking Educational Equity and Diversity (SEED) project by Wellesley Center for Women, Wellesley College, USA where he co-facilitates diversity workshops for educators.

Since 2015, Rohit has been working with Apni Shala in a variety of roles such has Youth SEL development, partnerships, communication and fundraising. In 2017, he co-founded Apni Shala's Khoj Community School, a project for whole-school approach to Social Emotional Learning with a focus on concept-based curriculum, multicultural education and community development.

Introduction

Hello and namaste,

Thank you for choosing to read my book.

I started writing it in August 2018 and it took me eight long months to bring it to its present form. I had just published my first book. Even after that, I felt like there was a lack of basic understanding of the subject. There are only a few people who know that mental health is important, but almost no one knows what mental health is. I completed the first draft of this book in November. Just as I was about to begin the publication process, I had the pleasure of reading *The God Delusion* by Richard Dawkins. The book had a huge impact on me as a writer. Dawkins explains complex arguments in simple terms and made them easy to understand. He also used statistics, logical reasoning and research to support his ideas on religion and atheism. As a writer, I felt inferior the moment I finished reading his book. I couldn't publish another book when books like these existed in the market. I remember ripping up the whole manuscript and then re-arranging it into the draft for this book.

I worked day and night. I missed college deadlines and had arguments over this book with my teachers and colleagues. It has taken a lot out of me, but I am convinced that it's in the best possible form now. I hope you gain insights from this book and appreciate the scale of the emergency we face. I hope it helps you understand what goes on in the mind of the mentally ill, and I hope it helps you become more knowledgeable and sensitive.

Happy reading.

Section I

From Possessed to Depressed

He was done with life.

Yashasvi, a 19-year-old boy found himself in a hotel room in the narrow streets of Bangalore in the summer of 2016. He had been living there for the past two months, pursuing an undergraduate degree. He was also suffering from severe clinical depression. For ethical reasons, the name of the patient has been changed.

People didn't really understand what depression felt like. He thought everyone mistook it for sadness or at worse, a lot of sadness. No one understood the numbness that comes along with it. Maybe people didn't understand; maybe he didn't want them to understand. He had received treatment from the National Institute of Mental Health and Sciences (NIMHANS) in Bangalore, one of the leading hospitals in India for the treatment of mental disorders, and another private hospital.

He sat there in his bed staring at the news on the TV. He didn't care one bit about what was on. The background noise of the news anchors provided a comforting obstacle to the train of thoughts in his head. Thoughts of suicide were making their way into his head again. He often wandered the roof of the hotel, wondering when he would finally make the jump. It wasn't because he felt sad, angry or frustrated, it was because he felt…nothing. The place where he felt emotions had been replaced by a black hole; it was where all emotions got sucked in, never to escape.

When he saw his family, he didn't feel happy. When he played football, the sport he loved, he didn't feel the peace that he had enjoyed in the past.

Nothing made him feel good.

Nothing made him feel bad.

Nothing made him feel.

It was like he was just going through the motions of life mechanically, without the feelings that coloured most people's perceptions. He often hurt himself because the physical pain made him feel something. In those 10 to 20 seconds, he felt something briefly. Even if it was terrible pain, he felt it and found a masochistic comfort in it.

It's a common belief that depression always has a cause. It's like depression demands a major tragedy before visiting someone. This wasn't the case with Yashasvi. When he first started feeling depressed, he was at the final peak of his school life. He had a close-knit group of friends and he had no major issues in his life, yet within two months of graduating from school, he found himself isolated, angry and self-destructive.

He was told it was a transient rebellious phase by some, characteristic of teenagers and that he would be fine within a few days. Others said that it was a quarter-life crisis, one that would resolve in weeks.

In reality, he ended up suffering from severe depression for two years. It took him two long years before he could start his prolonged recovery process, one that would take years.

Through this time, it became a common occurrence for him to receive unsolicited advice from people he knew only through his parents; people who claimed to have seen more in life than him.

"Change your city kid, and you will be fine in a jiffy."

"Eat some garlic and walk."

"Have some more water."

"Be responsible."

"Lose some weight."

"Focus on your career."

"Go out in the sun more."

This led Yashasvi to believe that his problems were geographical, nutritional, physiological, social and everything but psychological. It also made him wonder what sort of issues the previous generation faced if they could be solved by eating garlic!

Unfortunately, people tend to attribute behaviour that isn't normal to temporary problems. They like to believe an emotional problem can be solved by conditions that are easily altered. They think it is hard to change a person's mental state and avoid the idea that a problem could be psychological, as in Yashasvi's case.

People need to be open to the possibility that a persistently deviant behaviour, thought process or emotion may be due to psychological factors while considering other possibilities. They avoid it completely because of the shame attached with it. Claiming that someone has psychological problems immediately brings about labels like 'crazy,' 'unstable,' 'dangerous' and 'psychotic.' This is something that obviously needs to change, and we will discuss how we can change it throughout this book.

To Yashasvi, it was clear that this numbness was not a temporary guest but a permanent resident in his mind. It was there when he woke up and when he went to sleep. It was there when he did things he loved and when he performed mundane tasks. Transient despair was something he actually enjoyed; at least he felt some emotion in those moments.

He wasn't alone in feeling this way. At any moment, there are 45 million other Yashasvis across various parts of India. All of them going through the same numbness and vacuum. All of them being told to get over their problems. All of them (although I hope not) being asked to eat some garlic. At a global level, this figure becomes 322 million, marginally lower than the population of the United States of America. Depression is one of the 297 mental disorders recognized by the American Psychological Association and one of over 300 recognized by the World

Health Organization (WHO). If the stigma attached to something as common as clinical depression is so great, we can only estimate how great the stigma surrounding other, more poorly understood mental illnesses like schizophrenia, bipolar disorder, anorexia etc. must be.

Before we go further, there is something important I need to share with you. This book is a Psychology book. It is not a self-help book. Popular Psychology literature today has become one with self-help. Psychology isn't just about helping yourself or influencing others. It is much more than that.

Psychology is the scientific study of human behaviour, emotions and thought (cognitive) processes. It is a scientific endeavour to understand human behaviour, thinking and emotions. A discipline that tries to understand how the mind works. One that tries to explain how a person functions alone or in a group. Mental health is a discipline within Psychology.

We will return to Yashasvi's story later. We will see his story and that of many other people who have been afflicted with mental illnesses. Mental disorders are real conditions that affect real people with real lives. I will give you a look at how damaging they are. I will unlock the door to the mental health movement and leave it ajar. The decision to open it and enter this completely new world is solely yours.

A few months ago, I was having a pleasant discussion with a family friend on the political developments in India. The conversation slowly veered towards my work on mental health awareness and how the whole concept of mental disorders developed. As we talked, he said something I had heard often enough, "Arjun, I will be honest. In my times and in the times of my father, there was no such thing like depression or autism or all the terms you use today."

I smiled the moment I realized where this was going.

"If people were sad, they got over it. They didn't need labels to feel better about themselves. I don't mean to offend you, but I feel that these 'illnesses' are a modern invention of pharmacists to make money." He concluded.

Conspiracy theories have a certain appeal to them. Sadly for my friend, the conspiracy theory that depression is a modern illness is a verifiably false one. The presence of mental illnesses has been recorded in ancient texts across continents and cultures. In pre-historic times, it was mostly believed that mental illnesses were caused by the devil and were a fight between good and evil. Those who didn't have mental illnesses were *good* and those who did were possessed by spirits and demons. They were hence, chained and beaten very often.

The Greek thinker Hippocrates, in 400 BCE (after whom, a doctor takes his oath in the present day), was among the first people to try and change this perception. He said that mental illnesses were caused by biological factors rather than by spirits.

Ancient Indian texts (1500–500 BCE) provide accounts of the prevalence of mental illnesses too. They are probably the oldest of their kind. While most of Indian texts profess that mental illnesses are caused due to the spoiling of the soul (or the mind), the Atharva-veda, one of the four Vedas, said that mental disorders are the result of divine curses (Nizamie & Goyal, 2010). Texts like the Mahabharata and Ramayana also have various references to people who showed signs of mental illnesses. (Weiss, 1986; Bhugra, 1992)

A very popularly quoted example of depression in India comes from the Bhagavada Gita. People believe that a conversation between Lord Krishna and Arjuna, the warrior prince, are a perfect example of the counselling of a depressed person. The prototype of a depressed person in the mind of many Indians is the state of Arjuna just before he went into battle against his mentors and cousins. Arjuna was conflicted about what he was about to do. He did not want to kill his teachers and cousins. Neither did he want to shy away from his duty. For many people now, that is what depression is – being conflicted.

The work of Krishna for Arjuna is a typical example of crisis intervention through counselling (Nizamie & Goyal, 2010). Unfortunately, it has also led to many misconceptions about what counselling is like. Some people believe that counselling is a monologue that provides divine knowledge carrying the power to heal instantly. When a person visits a psychologist for the first time with these expectations, they are surprisingly disappointed.

In reality, a visit to a counsellor or therapist in search of healing must be a dynamic meeting. Both the patient and the counsellor need to engage in a dialogue on the patient's thoughts and how they can be managed in a better way. The client does most of the talking. A counsellor's job is to direct this conversation.

Yashasvi admitted that he had not been cooperative with his first few psychiatrists. He gave them the answers they wanted and projected the appearance of mental wellness. He kept waiting for a magical cure for his problems which simply did not exist.

The idea of mental illnesses being caused by biological factors was established by the work of Hippocrates and other Greek philosophers. The tide changed with the fall of the Roman empire in 476 CE. The fall led to Europe being dragged into the Dark Ages from 500 to 1400 CE. The church was at the forefront of everyday lives. Priests were given immeasurable power since they promised entry to heaven. This led to people with mental illnesses being subjected to atrocities once again. They were chained, beaten and experimented on.

People who believed that the mind was the site of demonic possession, cut holes in the skulls of the mentally ill – a process called trephination. They thought it gave the evil spirits a path to escape through. The people on whom this surgery was done had to spend their lives with a hole in their skulls.

In the modern world, this technique is used to relieve pressure of a swollen brain. Thankfully, we have stopped using trephination as a technique to cure mental illnesses.

Europe was gripped by a Christian fervour to conquer the world and hence, came the infamous Crusades. Some scholars argue that at a time when holy wars were taking place, the mentally ill were demonized as tools of propaganda to promote inter-religious animosity. Lives were sacrificed; innocent lives that needed compassion and companionship ended in a brutal fashion. Little did they know the road was only going to get worse for the mentally ill.

While the crusades raged, a new housing facility was established in London, the Bethlem Hospital.

The Bedlam of Bethlem

There are many persons now living who can remember passing the gates of old Bethlem and hearing, as they passed, the cut of the lash and the screams of its victims.

– Mary Lamb, a famous English writer who was suffering from a mental illness (1796)

To emphasize how marginalized and ill-treated the mentally sick were, you just need to take a look at the facilities they were housed in. These so-called facilities were hospitals only in name; everyone accepted that these places were prisons designed to keep *those people* inside.

The most infamous example is the Bethlem Hospital, which was opened in London in 1247. Despite being called a hospital; it was more of a public lodging where people could stay if they had no other place to sleep. The first reported use of this hospital as a care centre for the 'insane' was in the mid-13th century.

The manner in which they handled people was so atrocious that its name has become synonymous with neglect and chaos. The English word 'bedlam' which means 'a scene of uproar and confusion' finds its roots in the functioning of this hospital.

A hospital that was supposed to be among the first in the western world to take care of the mentally sick ended up leaving a legacy of ignorance and became a symbol of negligence.

From being a home to beggars and the homeless, Bethlem Hospital was transformed into a hospital for the mentally ill. At some point in the 17th century, two sections were created for the *melancholic* and the *lunatics*. The patients, or inmates, of the hospital were subjected to various treatments and therapies that were unconventional at best and cruel at worst.

One of those therapies was rotational therapy. The patient was suspended from a ceiling and rotated at high speeds, sometimes reaching 100 rotations a minute. This led to extreme vertigo and vomiting, which was considered a form of healing at the time. Other forms of healing included cupping therapy, exposure to leeches, ice baths, inducing blisters and regular beatings. At one point, the hospital refused to take in patients who were considered too weak to withstand the treatment. Indeed, many patients didn't make it.

Recently, mass graves have been discovered on the grounds of the old Bethlem Hospital. The dead were buried with proper rituals at first, but when the cemetery grew overcrowded they started piling coffins on top of the previous ones. When these coffins got too close to the surface, they abandoned the rituals altogether and dumped the dead bodies in a mass grave.

In the late 17th century, the staff at Bedlam went a step further in humiliating the mentally sick. They offered people a chance to see the mentally ill for money.

People could enjoy the animals in a zoo and then walk a few paces down the road to see the mentally insane in their natural habitat. Thomas Tyron, an English merchant and an author of popular self-help books was the first one to raise his voice against this novel form of humiliation. The only problem was that he was okay with displaying the patients for money; he just didn't want them to be displayed on holidays. It seems he had his priorities set straight.

This move may seem controversial and inhuman but there were other, contradictory aspects to this view as well. When the patients were put on public display, the fee charged for entry ended up contributing to the funding of the hospital. The administration frequently sought eminent personalities to visit the hospital in order to attract a larger audience. This led to more funds. This public exposure of patients also left the hospital administration open to public scrutiny. This meant that the caretakers could not be as brutal as they were earlier since any evidence of mistreatment would raise major concerns among people. It has been noted that the worst brutalities occurred immediately after the public left and once the crowds faded, the practice was discontinued completely.

In the 1800s, there was a lunacy reform movement across England and a parliamentary committee was set up to investigate the treatment of the patients at the, now notorious, Bethlem Hospital. One of the investigators, Edward Wakefield, a leading advocate of the Lunacy Reform, visited the hospital multiple times and made the following observations,

> *One of the side rooms contained about 10 [female] patients, each chained by one arm to the wall; the chain allowing them merely to stand up by the bench or form fixed to the wall, or sit down on it. The nakedness of each patient was covered by a blanket only ... Many other unfortunate women were locked up in their cells, naked and chained on straw ... In the men's wing, in the side room, six patients were chained close to the wall by the right arm as well as by the right leg ... Their nakedness and their mode of confinement gave the room the complete appearance of a dog kennel.*
>
> **– Edward Wakefield, 1814**

During the first few decades of the 19th century, a new mode of treatment, moral treatment was taking root across asylums in Europe. The idea had its roots in France and called for empathetic and compassionate treatment of the mentally ill. Despite the idea being popular across England, it was a shocking revelation for the general public when the news of the mistreatment of patients broke. It is no wonder that the initial attempts to visit Bethlem by Wakefield were rebuffed as the authorities wanted to maintain their image at a time when they were in dire need of funds.

Since those times, Bethlem has transformed and found its tumultuous way to the modern psychiatric era. Today, the focus has moved to treating patients with therapy and drugs instead of beatings and leeches. Recently, the hospital built a museum to display the patient's artwork and give a human touch to the otherwise de-humanized patients.

There have also been various attempts at re-interpreting the history of the hospital. To those trying to re-write history to fit their narratives, I say, history may be written by the victors but simply re-writing history, doesn't make you victorious.

The hospital, despite having over 750 years of history and lessons, continues to be a source of controversy and is actively avoided by many people seeking treatment.

Bethlem Hospital has changed over the centuries, but the bedlam has remained.

A Divine Intervention

It was a February day when Western psychiatry changed forever. Joan-Gilabert Jofré, a pastor in Valencia, Spain in 1409 was walking through the streets when he saw a commotion taking place in the distance. He saw some children teasing an elderly man.

"Madman, madman!" cried the youngsters as they giggled at the man's misery. They hit him occasionally and pelted small stones at him drawing pleasure from his incapacity. Father Jofré decided to intervene and helped the poor man.

He had been on various missions to rescue Christian missionaries from their Muslim captors. In those Mediterranean lands of North Africa, he had heard about how the mentally ill were treated in the Arab world (Moreno and colleagues, 2009). He heard accounts from Christians prisoners suffering from Pellagra, about how they were treated in hospitals for the mentally ill. There, they were treated with respect and care, and not chained up. It was this knowledge that made Father Jofré step in front of the mob.

He stood there like a wall between the old man and the children, his arms outstretched as the old man hid behind him for cover. Jofré appeared like divine intervention for the man. The mob quickly scattered and two days later, he delivered a sermon that changed how Westerners saw the mentally ill.

It was in March 1409 when Jofré delivered this sermon, two days after he protected the old man; he called for a place to stay for those who had lost their ability to reason. His exact words were,

In this city, there are many and very important pious and charitable initiatives. However, one very necessary one is lacking, that is, a hospital or house where the innocent and frenzied would be drawn together because many poor, innocent and frenzied people wander through this city. They suffer great hardships of hunger and cold and harm, because due to their innocence and rage, they do not know how to earn their living, nor ask for the maintenance they need for their living. Therefore, they sleep in the streets and die from hunger and cold and many evil persons, who do not have God in their conscience hurt them and point to where they are sleeping, they injury and kill and abuse some innocent women. It also occurs that the frenzied poor hurt many of the persons who are out wandering through the city. These things are known in the entire city of Valencia. Thus, it would be a very holy thing and work for Valencia to build a hostel or hospital where such insane or innocent persons could be housed so that they would not be wandering through the city and could not hurt nor be hurt.

This sermon was attended by an influential merchant, Lorenzo Salom who, along with other merchants and craftsmen, took the task of building the first psychiatric hospital in the western world. Spain came to be known as the cradle of western psychiatry.

The hospital was named after the Innocent Martyr Sons, who were a part of Christian mythology. In the Christian New Testament, Herod, the King of Judea had ordered all male children below the age of two, within the vicinity of Bethlem, be killed. The sons were too young to reach the age of reason and therefore, couldn't understand the concept of sin. They were allowed into heaven as the first martyrs of Christianity. Jofré professed that like these children, those who had lost their ability to reason could reach heaven in the afterlife as well.

While Bedlam Hospital was re-used to treat the mentally ill, its first purpose was as a house for the poor. Consequently, the first real Western psychiatric hospital was proposed in the humble streets of Valencia, Spain in the early 15th century and it was built by 1410. The hospital was named, The Hospital D'Innocents, Follcs I Orats (Hospital of The Innocents, The Insane and The Lunatics).

Father Jofré's actions were immortalized by the artist Joaquin Sorolla Bastida in 1887. The painting is considered an influential image in psychiatry.

Religion, despite all the cruelties it had imposed on the mentally sick earlier, ended up being an antecedent to the first psychiatric hospital in the western world. History is full of similar instances where religious figures have used their God's name for evil. Other people have used the name of the same God for kindness and service to mankind.

Atrocities have been committed in the name of God and continue to be as people fight over who has a better imaginary being. The fight between and within religions is ultimately fruitless and only holds humanity back.

Men like Jofré can be found in every religion around the world. Maybe it is not God who makes us evil or good, perhaps it is us who impose these roles on our Gods. It is time we started caring more about the people we can see right in front of us instead of fighting about beings that do not exist.

The Newton of Psychiatry

I cannot but give enthusiastic witness to their moral qualities. Never, except in romances, have I seen spouses more worthy to be cherished, more tender fathers, passionate lovers, purer or more magnanimous patriots, than I have seen in hospitals for the insane, in their intervals of reasonableness and calm; a man of sensibility may go there any day and take pleasure in scenes of compassion and tenderness.

– Phillipe Pinel

Despite the progressive steps taken in the streets of Valencia, it was not until the late 18th century that there was a real change in how the mentally ill were treated. In the last two decades of the 18th century, there was more focus on their treatment instead of their imprisonment.

The idea of treatment of the mentally sick has its roots in the French revolution of 1789. In March 1790, a decree proclaimed that all the people who had been imprisoned for their political views, religious blasphemy or mental incapability were to be released within six weeks. The mentally ill would be examined and either set free or taken care of in mental hospitals. While guillotines were cutting off heads and peasants were being told to eat cake, a physician was slowly changing how the insane were treated.

Philippe Pinel was born into a medical family on April 20, 1745 in the French township of Jonquières. He was the first of seven children. A kind young man, Pinel was considered an ideal candidate for priesthood. He moved to Toulouse at the age of 22 to study theology. There he came under the influence of Voltaire and other Enlightenment thinkers. In 1770, Pinel decided to follow in his father's footsteps.

Rather than studying for the priesthood, he began studying medicine, and received a doctorate in 1773. Pinel moved to Paris five years later. He was refused permission to practice medicine in France's capital because his medical degree was from a smaller university. He found means to earn a living in Paris, as a medical writer. In 1784, he was appointed the editor of the *Gazette de santé – The Health Journal*.

It was a personal loss that made him enter the world of mental illnesses – a friend's suicide. A friend had earlier approached him to help with his manic-depressive disorder. Soon after, he ran into the jungle and was eaten by wolves. This incident affected Pinel so much that he started working on ways to help people suffering from mental illnesses. He began writing about mental illness for the *Gazette de santé* and he also secured employment in a private asylum where he could study severe mental illness more thoroughly.

The French Revolution began in 1789 and helped Pinel's career. Two hospitals, Bicêtre and Saltpietre, were being used for the treatment of the mentally ill at the time. Pinel was put in charge of handling the treatment in Bicêtre in 1793, a Paris hospital that accommodated 4,000 patients including 200 categorized as insane. In the 1700s, it was normal practice to restrain mentally ill people by chaining them to the walls of hospitals or asylums. It is often said that Pinel freed the patients at Bicêtre from their restraint chains. Although he always credited the Governor of the hospital, Jean-Baptiste Pussin for this move. Regardless, a sort of legend was created about Pinel liberating the insane. This is actually a myth.

Having previously worked in an asylum, Pinel was interested in seeing how mentally ill patients were treated at Bicêtre. There he encountered Jean-Baptiste Pussin, the head of the mental ward. Pussin was managing patients in a manner that Pinel had not seen before.

In 1790, three years before Pinel arrived, Pussin had ordered patients' chains removed. Some of them had been chained for decades. He also prohibited violence against the patients. It is said that this legend was created by his son, Scipion Pinel.

Pinel Jr. was angry that his father was focussing on psychological factors instead of biological ones. He meant to spread the rumour to discredit his father, but he ended up earning his father the title of Father of Modern Psychiatry.

Pinel once told a patient with a history of violence, who had been at Bicêtre for 40 years, that he would like to take his chains off. Pinel asked him if he would be non-violent. He promised. Pinel unchained him. The patient went out into the sunlight for the first time in many years. He exclaimed how beautiful the light was. He remained calm, helped other inmates, and was released two years later (India Today, 2017).

Instead of chaining his patients up and beating them, Pinel treated the sick with compassion and care. He often visited his patients multiple times in a day and had therapeutic conversations with them. He talked to them about their thoughts and feelings and offered a sense of comfort and trust that was previously missing. This method was called moral treatment.

Pinel's views were also displayed by how he talked about the mentally ill and how they were seen at the time. He looked at his patients as humans and not as possessed by devils or spirits. His contributions to the world of psychiatry are legendary. Some scholars go so far as to say that his work was on level with Newton's equations to Science and Linnaeus to Taxonomy.

Pinel's work was not limited to better treatment of the mentally ill. He was considered the greatest authority on internal healthcare at the time and considered one of the forefathers of the idea of a list of all mental disorders. It was called the Philosophical Classification of Diseases and was published in 1798. Since then, the idea of classifying mental disorders has caught on.

Pinel's classification is considered the ancestor of the modern International Classification of Diseases, a classification directory that is maintained by the WHO and lists various criteria for diagnosing a mental disorder. His career was full of innovations and academic work that has served as a precursor to multiple modern methods of medicine.

On 25 October 1826, at the age of 81, Pinel passed away after a battle with pneumonia. He was buried in a cemetery in Paris. The funeral was attended by state dignitaries, doctors, scientists and the patients he had attended to at Bicêtre and Saltpetre.

One of the people attending his funeral was a man who had a history with violence. His fondest memory of Pinel was when the doctor took off his chains, let him walk in the sunlight and made him realize how beautiful the light was.

A Freudian Leap

I have found my tyrant, and in his service I know no limits. My tyrant is Psychology. It has always been my distant, beckoning goal and now since I have hit upon the neuroses, it has come so much the nearer.

– Sigmund Freud in a letter to Wilhelm Fliess, 1895

Sigmund Freud.

One of the most recognizable names in Psychology.

There has been a cult around the man for quite some time now. Ever since he put forward his ideas, he has been heavily criticized and ardently supported. He was the main force in Psychology in the first half of the 20th century. Today, most of his theories are in ruins yet his supporters continue to believe that the man changed how people thought of Psychology. Indeed, mental disorders were not shielded from his influence.

Freud was fascinated by the discovery that there were some sensations which went unnoticed by our consciousness. He believed that the consciousness was just one part of the human psyche while the major part of it was our unconscious mind. A concept he was the first to formalize. His iceberg model of the mind said that the conscious experience is merely the tip of the iceberg.

He believed that there are many experiences that do not enter our conscious mind but stay in our unconscious. For him, the unconscious was the part of the iceberg that is underwater and is never accessed or seen. In between these two was the subconscious mind, which was partly above water and partly below it.

The child is the father of the man.

– William Wordsworth, 1802

Freud believed that as a child, there are many experiences which ultimately shape our personality and decide the kind of life one is going to lead in the future. These experiences may not necessarily stay in our memory or conscious mind, but they affect our behaviour through the unconscious mind. After the advent of moral treatment, the next major step came roughly a century later when Freud explained the mechanisms of the mind and how they influence personality.

Moral treatment had spread like wildfire across Europe and America. The mentally sick were no longer chained but treated with compassion and trust. There was a debate on whether the causes of mental illness were biological or psychological. At the very least, there was a consensus that they were not caused supernaturally.

As moral treatment developed, it emerged that this treatment was causing people to become too attached to their doctors. The patients could not stay calm without seeing their doctors for an extended period. This attachment developed into an unhealthy habit. This was also when the first predecessors of psychopharmacology developed. People were using opioids to treat melancholia and other psychological disorders.

Freud believed that mental illnesses were the manifestation of our unconscious urges and needs. He believed that a dream was a symbolic manifestation of our unconscious and could be used to treat mental illnesses. He used dream analysis to understand a patient's unconscious mind. It helped him understand what was troubling their psyche. These symbolic representations were often exaggerated.

For example, if a person had low self-esteem, they would dream about being shamed in public or if they were feeling warm, they would dream about being stuck in a house on fire.

Freud proposed another idea – free association. He said it could uncover the feelings of the unconscious. This concept is popular in mainstream culture today albeit not with the same name and in a slightly different form.

In the Bollywood movie, *Zindagi Na Milegi Dobara*, there is a scene when Imran, the poet, is sitting in the backseat of the car looking contemplative. His friend, Kabir notices this and proposes a simple test to understand what is troubling him. The third friend, Arjun, watches on. Kabir says that he will say some words and Imran must say whatever comes to his mind immediately. Imran complies. He pauses when he hears the word, "father."

This is a word association test, which was developed by Freud's student Carl Jung. In the movie, the three friends later find out that Imran struggled with the thought of meeting his father who abandoned him at a young age. Freud believed that when the conscious mind is not given any time to repress the unconscious, it is easier to see its manifestations.

In the 1880s–90s, the term 'melancholia' was replaced by 'depression' by Adolf Meyer. While today it might seem like a redundant act, at that time it was very significant. There is a persistent myth among people that there are some people who are just depressed all the time and they are pessimistic by nature. These people are pessimistic and are said to have a melancholic temperament. They are not necessarily depressed throughout life, but they are more likely to fall into the dark pit of depression. The renaming of melancholia to depression made it easier to distinguish between the melancholic temperament and the depressive disorder. But do we, the great *homo sapiens*, ever learn that easily?

The distinction has again lost its meaning today. People have started using 'depression' as a transient mood or feeling instead of a disorder.

This has led to the use of 'clinical depression' to distinguish between the mood and the illness.

The description and terminology used by Freud influenced psychiatric care for a long time. Freud's work still divides and inspires people. His life was full of stories about abandonment, anger, regret and stubbornness. When Freud was at the peak of his career, he was diagnosed with mouth cancer. Being a stubborn man, he continued to smoke 20 cigars a day. In 1939, he lived every day in terrible pain. He asked his physician for some help. He did not want to suffer anymore. The physician, a close friend, fulfilled his last wish. Sigmund Freud died via assisted suicide on 23 September 1939. Thus, the story of the most influential psychologist of all time came to an end.

The Wounded Revolutionary

For of what account are truth and love when life itself has ceased to seem desirable?

– Clifford Whittingham Beers

In the last decade of the 19th century and the first of the 20th, there was an awakening across psychologists and psychiatrists in the UK and USA regarding the plight of psychiatric patients. It was known as the 'mental hygiene movement.' Around the same time, a young man named Clifford Whittingham Beers was being admitted to a mental hospital in Connecticut, USA. This man would go on to change how we look at mental health forever.

Clifford Beers was born in 1876 in Connecticut, USA. His parents had gone through multiple tragedies in their lives. They lost a child in its infancy. Another child of theirs developed seizures as a teenager and died. Beers was worried that he may develop the same condition with age. He was one of three children who made it to adulthood. The other two had spent time in mental asylums and died by suicide there. While pursuing an undergraduate degree, Beers developed severe depression. He managed to graduate in 1897 despite this hardship. He worked in New York but became increasingly depressed. On returning to his family home in 1900, he tried to kill himself by jumping out of his bedroom window.

Between 1900–1903, he was admitted to three different psychiatric hospitals. In all three hospitals, he suffered physical abuse, humiliation and mistreatment. He compiled his experiences in a book that he released in 1908, *A Mind That Found Itself.*

The impact of the book was instantaneous. It was favourably reviewed, well accepted and is in print even today. This led to the formation of the Mental Hygiene Society in 1908 and in the next year, the National Committee for Mental Hygiene was founded thanks to the efforts of Meyer and Beers. This led to the formation of the International Committee on Mental Hygiene, which was later superseded by the World Federation of Mental Health.

In the 1930s, the aim of the Committee shifted from curative to preventive measures. The focus of the shift was that they needed to take mental healthcare to the common man and make it more accessible. It was believed that a more aware and sensitized society could play a role in the improved management of mental illnesses. In late 1930s, some radical ideas like eugenics and sterilization of the mentally ill gained some traction. This coincided with the rise of Adolf Hitler and his beliefs of a supreme race, but they were soon discarded.

The First International Conference of Mental Hygiene was held in London in 1948, but by the time it ended the term 'mental hygiene' found itself replaced by the modern word, 'mental health.'

In the 1950s, there was another shift in perspective in mental healthcare. Mental health was no longer seen as simply the absence of mental illnesses. It was believed that it was necessary to have a positive outlook on mental health and a new definition was sought.

Beers got married in 1912, but the couple decided not to have any children. They were wary of any genetic propagation of mental illnesses.

Beers was not a psychiatrist or a doctor in any sense of the word. However, he was highly honoured by psychiatric associations across the USA. The state of mental health we see today is based on a large contribution from Clifford Beers' work.

His life is a testament to how life throws many challenges at us and, how gaining knowledge from them and improving from them can help change the society. In the 1930s, his association was struggling for funds and his brothers had died. Beers was understandably overwhelmed. He sought admission at a mental hospital to ensure his well-being. Sadly, he died four years later of pneumonia in the same hospital. He was 67-years-old at the time.

His legacy lives on. His work has ensured the presence of mental health in mainstream discourse in the USA. Today, Mental Health America exists only because of his work. Their main aim is to promote mental health awareness and ensure the ethical treatment of psychiatric patients is carried out. One man's misery, suffering and subsequent tenaciousness saved the lives of thousands.

* * *

Not only is the concept of mental health a very old one, it comes with a rich history. We see humanity at its absolute worst and also its compassionate best. We go through the major developments from prehistoric thinkers and then move on to how easily mental health care can be morph into the cruel detention and dehumanization of patients. The history of mental health is not just a long story, but also a very diverse one. It touches on the developments of the French revolution as well as the royal family of England.

We focussed mostly on a west-centred approach to the history of mental health care. Nevertheless, we must not forget that there were great developments taking place in the east in China and India as well.

The advances in technology and knowledge made over time sadly do not always convert into actual change. The human rights of the mentally sick continue to be a major challenge in various parts of the world. While they are provided with rights by law, reality tells a different tale.

On 6th August 2001, 26 patients died in a fire in a mental home in Erwada, a pilgrimage site in South India. These people were tied to poles by their legs and they had no chance of getting out. When they shouted to be saved, their cries were ignored as it was believed to be customary ranting. After the fire was doused, some bodies could not even be identified. The patients were chained up because everyone thought they were possessed. Some thought the fire took place to punish these 'evil' patients. Today, the tragedy is a forgotten one in India. We are never short of tragedies due to administrative failure any way. Those 26 lives, their painful end, their screams, their cries, they all count for nought.

The life of the mentally ill is cheap, after all.

Section II

Defining Mental Health

A major barrier that stops people from spreading awareness about mental health, is the question of how mental health is defined. Laymen have various definitions which are not the same for everyone. There is little agreement on a general definition for 'mental health' and currently, there is widespread use of the term 'mental health' as a euphemism for 'mental illness'. (Manwell, 2015)

While it is considered by many to be an absence of mental illness, there are people who disagree. The absence of sadness is not happiness and not being ill does not always mean being healthy. Mental health has very blurred lines at the moment; the boundaries cut across subjects like Psychology, Neurology and interestingly, Spirituality.

Mental health today is interwoven with Psychology. It is believed that only two types of people are talking about mental health (1) those who have a background in Psychology or (2) those who have suffered from a mental illness themselves. For a meaningful change to take place, this notion needs to change. People need to be introduced to the idea of mental health and how it can affect their daily life.

Psychology needs to widen its horizons and reach out to the public as well. There is a lot of confusion about what the subject matter of Psychology as a discipline is. Some people think that it is only about reading people's minds or brainwashing them. Psychology is much more than that. It tries to understand why people behave the way they do, what makes them more intelligent than others, how the same amount of pain is felt by different people and how people make a decision in isolation versus in a group to name a few. It is not only a study of mental illnesses; it is a study of the mind.

Psychology, in comparison to Physics or Chemistry, is a young science. It is not an exact science and is open to different definitions of a concept as time passes. Physics, on the other hand is much more precise. You can predict the trajectory and landing position of a ball if you know the value of certain variables. In Psychology, you cannot always predict how a person thinks or will respond to a situation.

When we define a concept or an idea in Physics, it is precise and goes through very few changes over time. Take the example of the atom. Ancient thinkers (around 400 BCE) believed that the atom was an indivisible unit, and everything was built from atoms. This view changed centuries later with the discovery of the electron, proton and neutron. In the 19th century, it was believed that these three particles are indivisible, but the recent discovery of quarks in 1968 has again changed the way we look at the atom. These changes come once in centuries and once they are made, they are likely to remain unaffected for centuries to come. Things are a little different in Psychology. Here, the definitions of a concept change over decades with new research or different perspectives. One might ask then, how do psychologists decide which definition is the right one? The answer is that there is no real right answer. Social sciences do not have a right answer.

Ask yourself, "Why have there been so may wars throughout history?"

A feminist might say that it is because of men who are always greedy for more power. An atheist may say that it is due to every religion's inherent call for violence. A Marxist may say that it is due to capitalism. And an Indian may say that it is because of white imperialism. None of these answers are wrong and none of these are right. There have been many wars fought over religion and many fought over money. Almost all of them have various reasons, this only complicates the matter further. The truth is that the answer depends on how you see the world. It depends on how you have been raised and what you have been taught starting from your childhood. There is no single right answer. Everyone is living their own reality.

This existence of multiple realities makes it harder to define any psychological concept. The 'rightest' any definition can be is one that holds true across different realities, cultures and times. At any given time, the definitions of psychological concepts are not necessarily the same across cultures. A kilogram weighs the same in India, the USA and Colombia but a psychological concept may have different definitions and understandings based on different cultures.

A good example to help you understand this variation is the concept of intelligence. We use the word 'intelligence' very often in our daily lives, but questions that are rarely asked include:

What is intelligence?

Who decides who is intelligent and who is not?

Is academics the only dimension to intelligence?

A concept like intelligence had to go through many definitions as well. Earlier, people believed that those who scored higher on a particular test were more intelligent than their peers. The government of France tried to differentiate between children who were slow learners from normal students. Alfred Binet (1905), a psychologist at the time, was given the job of devising a way to establish this differentiation. He came up with the first test for intelligence. Binet is also the one to be blamed for the IQ tests we face today.

He devised the words idiots, morons and imbeciles. They were to be used to refer to people with lower than average intelligence. Idiots are people who have an IQ from 0–25. Imbeciles have an IQ between 26–51 and morons have an IQ between 51–70. After all, it is important you know your insults.

Even in today's world, IQ is considered the main parameter to measure intelligence and used as a predictor of success in life, but intelligence does not always equal success. IQ only measures some aspects of our thinking processes. It is harsh to say that those who do not fit into this narrow description of intelligence are not smart.

In 1983, Howard Gardner, an American psychologist, proposed that a population has multiple intelligences. Gardner was the son of Jewish refugees from Nazi Germany. He was a studious child who loved to read, and while he had originally planned to study Law, he chose to study Developmental Psychology as he was influenced by the work of Jean Piaget. He was also mentored by the famous psychoanalyst, Erik Erikson and this contributed to his decision to pursue Psychology.

The biggest mistake of past centuries in teaching has been to treat all students as if they were variants of the same individual and thus, to feel justified in teaching them all the same subjects the same way (Howard Gardner in Siegel & Shaughnessy, 1994).

My mind was really opened when I went to Harvard College and had the opportunity to study under individuals — such as psychoanalyst Erik Erikson, sociologist David Riesman, and cognitive psychologist Jerome Bruner — who were creating knowledge about human beings. That helped set me on the course of investigating human nature, particularly how human beings think (Howard Gardner quoted by Marge Sherer, 1999).

These intelligences, he proposed, are not just limited to the abilities of Logic and Mathematics. They include concepts like verbal intelligence, visuo-spatial intelligence, kinaesthetic intelligence, interpersonal and intrapersonal intelligences, etc. He proposed that it is not necessary for everyone who was bad at Mathematics to be un-intelligent. They could be intelligent in some other form.

If you judge a fish by its ability to climb a tree, it will spend its whole life thinking it is stupid.

While he didn't say these exact words, this quote does encapsulate his ideas well.

The problem with defining intelligence is that there are many different concepts of it across cultures. The people in Sweden may say that intelligence is about being able to create beautiful art or music, while a mother in India may say that her child is not intelligent because of his low marks in Mathematics. A person who does not always stick to the rules may say that being street-smart is being intelligent while a law-abiding citizen may say that following rules and laws requires intelligence. Hence, it becomes a bit tedious to have an all-encompassing definition for intelligence.

Overcoming these barriers, Robert Sternberg (1977, 1985, 1995, 2005) gave a different perspective on how intelligence is understood. Sternberg was an inept test taker due to test anxiety during his childhood. This upset him and he reasoned that a test was not an adequate measurement of his true knowledge and academic abilities. He said that;

Intelligence is the ability to achieve one's goals in life, given one's sociocultural context by capitalizing on strengths and correcting or compensating for weaknesses in order to adapt to, shape, and select environments, and through a combination of analytical, creative, and practical abilities.

– (Sternberg, 2005)

He also emphasized the importance of the cultural context of an intelligence test, when he said that intelligence is meaningless without a cultural context.

Most definitions before Sternberg's focused on just adapting to the environment. They said that if a person is able to adapt to their environment then they can be said to have some level of intelligence. Sternberg expanded on this idea by saying that it was not just about adapting to the environment but also knowing when to change your environment, that is, having the ability to select your environment. The boiling frog example will help you understand.

If we keep a frog in a bowl of water and heat it, the frog will use its energy adjusting to the temperature of the water. By the time the water begins to boil, the frog has already lost all its energy and is too weak to jump out of the bowl. The frog that kept adjusting to its environment and did not choose a better one when it could have, ended up dying and cannot be considered intelligent. Whereas, a frog that jumps out of the bowl before using too much energy on adapting is considered an intelligent one. This is because it has the ability to change its environment and select a better one when it is available.

Sternberg proposed three major components of intelligence (1) Analytical (2) Creative (3) Contextual. He said that someone who could critically analyze information is intelligent, but intelligence is not limited to analytical skills. According to him, intelligence is mostly about the ability to process information and what a person can do with various pieces of information. The ability to create information or organize it in novel ways (creative) or being able to choose the right information at the right time (contextual) is intelligence as well. An example would explain this better.

One day, a boy was walking through the park on a bright sunny afternoon. He saw a group of people forming a crowd near the fountain. He grew curious and joined them; a young man was playing the guitar. The boy liked the attention this man was getting and wanted to learn how to play the guitar too. When he saw the man playing the guitar, he received new information and decided that he wanted more of it. He started coming to the park every day, at the same time, to watch the guitarist play. The boy shrewdly observed the guitarist's finger movements and learned to recreate them to some extent. This ability to analyze his movements carefully is considered the analytical component of intelligence.

The boy then convinced his parents to get him a guitar. Once he got it, he practiced on it every day. With time, he learned to produce new sounds. This ability to create new knowledge out of previously learned knowledge is the creative component of intelligence. Now that he had achieved some level of mastery over the instrument, the young boy started playing the guitar in public spaces as well. He mostly played light-hearted tunes but when a funeral procession passed by one day, he stopped playing for some time. He stopped because he knew it was inappropriate to play a happy song while people grieve. This ability to use the knowledge we have in appropriate situations is the contextual component of intelligence.

While this is the currently the most accepted definition, it is always open to refinement and improvement, should an opportunity arise.

Another influence on any definition in behavioural sciences is the zeitgeist of the time, that is the spirit of the times. Think of it as the flavour of the atmosphere. For example, in today's times, nationalism is the zeitgeist. There are many discussions about it in the political world. Books are written on its intricacies and history, and movies are produced depicting nationalistic ideas. In academic circles, research that is considered to be in favour of national interests are encouraged and there is a focus on helping the nation.

Similarly, the definition of mental health used by psychologists has often been influenced by the school of Psychology that was dominant at the time. Going back to the definition of Psychology, it has three basic components – behaviour, emotions and cognitive processes. As we go through history, you will notice that over time, different emphasis has been put on the different aspects of this definition. Some have said that cognitive processes should be more important, and others have said that emotions and cognitive processes should not be studied *at all*.

The History of Psychology

Physics has been the elder brother Psychology has always tried to emulate. Behavioural scientists have long wanted Psychology to be more like its physical and life science counterparts, particularly the venerated science of Physics. (Hunt, 2005)

The zeitgeist of the pure sciences, especially Physics, has had a great influence on the birth as well as the development of Psychology. In the time of Newton, when the laws of motion were established, the philosophers of the time were amazed by how the motion of an object could be predicted, explained and described through simple mathematical equations. We do not really appreciate the significance of the discovery today but at the time, it changed how people looked at the environment that surrounded them. Science and Physics have been doing this to the human race for quite some time.

When Copernicus said that the Sun was the centre of the solar system and not the Earth, we realized that we were not so special. Galileo was executed by the church for saying the same thing! To know that the physical objects in our surroundings were following simple mathematical equations was surreal. This made people want to know what else could be simplified to equations. Some philosophers set out to decode the human mind and describe it through similar equations. This group of people ended up being the antecedents of modern Psychology and were called the 'associationists' in the 17th century.

The work of the associationists was followed by Willhelm Wundt. He was credited with establishing Psychology as a scientific discipline in 1879. He and his student, E.B. Titchener ended up being called 'structuralists.' They were mostly concerned with understanding the basic elements of the mind and our consciousness.

Titchener was a peculiar person to say the least.

He is said to have had an aura about him that made his students perform unsettling tasks at his direction. Once, he made his students swallow rubber tubes for the whole day and report on what they felt as they were fed in the Psychology lab. If that is not extreme enough, he even made his students record their sensations and emotions during intercourse! Titchener believed that in order to be a good psychologist, one needed to smoke, and he believed that women were too pure to smoke. This caused women to be left out of his 'closed' society, which was called 'Titchener's Experimentalists'. This makes him seem like a misogynist, but he also oversaw the Doctorates of many female scholars. He was also one of the first people to call for women to be allowed to deliver lectures, something that was considered heresy at the time.

Despite all the attention that Sigmund Freud gets, Psychology is full of personalities that stood apart during their time.

The development of 'functionalists' (who focused on the functions of the consciousness) after them continued the progress of Psychology. Structuralism played a very important role in the growth of the discipline of Psychology. It acted as an anchor that could be criticized and used to develop new theories and ideas. Functionalism was the first school of thought to emerge from this anchor. It emerged in 1898 through the work of William James.

The functionalists led to the formation of the American Psychological Association under the leadership of G. Stanley Hall (1892). They found the weight of the great Charles Darwin (1857) behind their thoughts. When the Theory of Evolution was put forward, Darwin claimed that every process in our body adapted to promote the survival of our species. This made the functionalists ask, "What is the purpose of having a conscious experience?"

At this time, the atom was found to no longer be indivisible. The discovery of the electron, proton and neutron brought about emphasis on the scientific nature of Psychology. During this period, a radical movement was developing. A movement that would wage a radical war against structuralism and functionalism. They were the behaviourists. They emerged in 1913 thanks to the work of John B. Watson.

They said that Psychology had been too focused on unobservable concepts like thoughts, emotions, etc. They stated that it only needed to study external, observable behaviour and nothing else. The subject matter of Psychology was a stimulus and how an individual responded. They did not care about why the individual behaved in this way. Pavlov and his dogs were the antecedents of this school of Psychology. When it was discovered that organisms can be conditioned or 'taught' to learn certain behaviours, the school of behaviourism really took off. They produced the concept of conditioning and dominated the field of Psychology for most of the 20th century.

When behaviourists were about to declare a radical war on the set assumptions of Psychology, Sigmund Freud (1900) set out on a separate path to illustrate how all our behaviour was determined by our experiences as a child.

He said that humans are innately sinful and directed by our unconscious urges. His school of thought was termed psychoanalysis and has since played an important role in therapy treatments and other forms of treatment for mental illnesses. Freud's life and the development of psychoanalysis was not free from drama. When he first proposed his theory of the psychosexual stages of child development (1905), there was plenty of controversy around it. Freud proposed that a child is shaped by their sexual needs and based on whether these needs are fulfilled or not determine the child's personality. Many prominent names abandoned Freud; they stated that something as innocent as an infant did not need to be sexualized. Carl Jung, the man who Freud saw as his 'heir apparent' and 'spiritual son,' left psychoanalysis to never return. Jung made his name in a separate field of psychology and the seat of Freud's heir was left empty.

In the 1950s, Psychology was mostly dominated and confined to the behaviourists academically. There was an air of cynicism about Psychology and everything seemed very pessimistic. At this time, Abraham Maslow came forth like a shining light. He said that Psychology had focussed on the ill for too long and needed to focus on what the healthy could achieve. He, along with Carl Rogers, set up a new school of psychology called Humanism.

I am deliberately rejecting our present easy distinction between sickness and health, at least as far as surface symptoms are concerned. Does sickness mean having symptoms? I maintain now that sickness might consist of not having symptoms when you should. Does health mean being symptom-free? I deny it. Which of the Nazis at Auschwitz or Dachau were healthy? Those with a stricken conscience or those with a nice, clear, happy conscience? Was it possible for a profoundly human person not to feel conflict, suffering, depression, rage, etc.?

– (Abraham Maslow, 1962).

Humanists were focused on fulfilling the potential of a human being and achieving the pinnacle of life. Maslow's Hierarchy of Needs continues to be a constant source of knowledge in various disciplines like management, sociology, etc. They proposed that mental health was not just about the absence of an illness but about achieving a person's full potential and contributing to society.

In the 1970s, there was a cognitive revolution where emphasis was put on the cognitive processes of the mind once again and in the 1990s, psychologists started looking into a neurological basis for Psychology. The focus was on the use of neurological techniques to understand the functioning of the mind. The invention of functional techniques like MRI and PET scans helped progress this area of study. This led to the development of Neuropsychology.

At the time of this book's writing (2019), Psychology is mostly focused on Positive Psychology (an offshoot of the humanist school) and Neuropsychology.

It is important that you understand that this is merely the history of Psychology, not its past. Psychological concepts like personality, intelligence, emotions and behaviour have been discussed very often in the texts of ancient cultures of Greece, India and China. Psychology as a scientific discipline started only in 1879, but it has a lot of literature ready in the ancient texts.

Psychology has a long past, but a short history. (Ebbinghaus, 1908)

Defining Mental Health

Over the years, many mental health activists have tried to initiate a conversation about mental health, but one frustrating thing that holds then back is not many understand *what* mental health is. A major obstacle for integrating mental health initiatives into global health programmes and healthcare services is a lack of consensus on a definition of mental health (Manwell & Roberts, 2015). As we have already discussed, psychological concepts are not very easy to define.

When asked to define what mental illness is, a common reply is mental illness, much like physical illness is being abnormal or displaying abnormal characteristics. An appropriate example would be the case of haemoglobin in blood, there is a defined range which is considered normal and any deviation from that, whether below or above normal is considered a sign of a disease. Mental illnesses, unfortunately, do not work that way.

They do not provide a physical manifestation, which can be tested against a population for normalcy. How do you test for an illness if it leaves no sign of its existence? Infectious diseases leave behind a fever and cancer leaves behind a change in the cytology of an individual. A mental disorder is not so kind to any of us.

It does not leave many, if any, physical traces behind. Another problem with this definition is who defines what is 'normal' or 'abnormal'? If someone has thoughts or emotions that do not match that of the normal population, do we end up calling them mentally ill? If it was so, psychiatrists would end up becoming 'social engineers' who could call any undesirable behaviour an illness and force people to conform to society. This concern about social engineering was one of the main criticisms of psychiatry in the 1960s. There was a strong anti-psychiatry movement in '60s and '70s. It was led by Dr. Thomas Szasz who we will talk about later in the book. The peak of the zeitgeist was the movie *One Flew Over the Cuckoo's Nest* where psychiatrists were seen forcing normalcy on their patients. The definition of mental health needs to shift its focus away from aligning with a population because populations change and always will. We need to have a definition of mental health which focuses on the individual instead of the people around them.

The Current Definition

Mental health is defined as a state of well-being in which every individual realizes his or her own potential, can cope with the normal stresses of life, can work productively and fruitfully, and is able to make a contribution to her or his community (WHO, 2001).

One look at the current definition of mental health used by the WHO shows clear influences from the humanistic school of Psychology. There is an emphasis on 'fulfilling his or her own potential' and 'contribution to community.' This definition is borrowed from another school of psychology called Positive Psychology. In very simple terms, it is humanist psychology but with an emphasis on empirical scientific evidence.

When Maslow first shared his ideas with the world, he was criticized for being too idealistic and not having any scientific evidence (Graham & Messner, 1998). It was believed that Maslow's work was appealing in theory, but it did not have anything to make it scientific. Despite many studies showing only rudimentary support in favour of the ideals of Humanism, the spectre of scientific evidence has haunted it forever.

Positive Psychology is the spirit of today's times, it is logical that it has a dominating influence on the perception of mental health.

In this model, mental health is portrayed as a utopian mind space where every human is at the maximum of their potential and possesses a 'good character.'

This definition, while currently in use, has many drawbacks and makes some common assumptions that are considered short-sighted by some. Marx, Nietzsche and Freud were the first to be critical when they said we cannot have too much emphasis on optimism as it colours our perception of reality. Being optimistic is a good thing but ignoring damning realities just to maintain a façade of optimism would be a grave mistake for anyone to commit.

Another drawback is that the definition of mental health is too broad. While it moves away from the idea that anyone not mentally ill is mentally healthy, it brings in other domains that are too wide for Psychology. How do we know if someone is working to their full potential? How do we know if someone is being as productive as they can be and why, oh why, must everyone be a useful member of the community to be considered mentally healthy?

Despite all these drawbacks, it is the definition currently used in Psychology. Consequently, most researchers have used this definition as the standard definition of mental health since its adoption in 2001. There are various concepts like emotional intelligence that do not make a large part of the modern definition of mental health. Resilience and emotional intelligence are the two most important concepts needed to form a mentally healthy society in my opinion.

Resilience

Resilience is a divisive topic among mental health advocates. The academicians working to increase mental health awareness often talk about the need for higher resilience. On the other hand, people who have suffered from mental illnesses and now advocate for mental health shy away from this topic. This may be because resilience is sometimes used to put people down. People incorrectly believe that those who have had mental illness lack resilience and therefore, must be weak. In a study by The Live Love Laugh Foundation (2018), a majority of respondents (60%) agreed with the statement that one of the main causes of mental illness is a lack of self-discipline and willpower.

Resilience is the quality that we use while tackling stressors in our lives. The current definition of mental health talks about 'coping with the normal stresses of life,' this can be considered a part of resilience. But it is not just about coping with normal stresses; it is about having the belief that we can cope with most of the stresses that we face in life.

Resilience continues to be an elusive concept for psychologists across the world. It has varied meanings and there is little consensus on a universal definition. Despite this, there are some people who unknowingly advocate the use of resilience in defining mental health. The most controversial among them is Piers Morgan, a British journalist.

On World Mental Health Day, 10 October 2018, Piers Morgan tweeted about how people and especially children need to be taught about mental resilience instead of mental health. His tweets regarding the subject read as follows;

I think it's time to change the language on 'mental health'. Let's start using the phrase 'mental strength' and teach our kids the power of resilience.

I'm not talking about serious things – clearly some people have genuine problems that need to be dealt with and treated, but some people have this anxiety and it seems to me there's this lack of training to be resilient.

Morgan says that teaching young children about the power of resilience is important to improve the state of mental health that the UK finds itself in today. The annoying thing was that he was not willing to talk about 'serious things' as he put it. He does not deny the fact that some people have genuine problems but is not willing to talk about them. Why?

Many people do not understand that the 'serious things' that people have, develop from the normal mood changes of life. Disorders like Major Depressive Disorder or Anxiety Disorder mostly start with a prolonged sadness or nervousness that eventually develops into a disorder. This is why mental illnesses are scary. They can happen to anyone at any time. If we do not catch them at the right time, it could lead to harmful consequences. Giving young children training in resilience would be a preventive measure instead of a curative one and yes, prevention is better than cure, but the problem is that it does not address the problems of those who are already going through these things.

Morgan then suggested that we replace the term 'mental health' with 'mental strength.' There are a myriad of reasons why that would be an unwise move. Mental strength carries with it the connotation that those who are not able to deal with a stressor in life are 'weak.' People who suffer from mental illnesses are already considered as those with 'weak will power.' This common belief leads to patients internalizing these mistaken beliefs.

If everyone around you thinks you are weak, after a certain point, you will start believing you are weak too. Using 'strength' instead of 'health' will only make this process of self-stigmatization quicker.

Another important distinction here is that while children should be taught about solving problems individually with the aid of surrounding resources, it is equally important that we tell them what to do if they cannot solve the problem alone. We need to tell them techniques they could use or improvements they could make to their current strategies in order to solve problems efficiently. It is important that we believe in our abilities to tackle stressors in order to be mentally healthy. Morgan failed to understand that serious mental problems become serious only when we do not treat them at the right time.

It is important that we take care of the severely ill, support the mildly ill and teach the vulnerable techniques to tackle their problems.

There is another reason I included these tweets. They generated a lot of vile abuse. Many people called him 'tone deaf' and others said that he was denigrating people suffering from mental illnesses; he was going so far as to call them weak. Over time, Morgan has created an aura of being the devil's advocate. I decided to include these tweets because it was something that needed to be talked about. It also exposed some glaring flaws in how people perceive mental health awareness currently.

Morgan simply stated that he wants people to be taught about mental resilience instead of mental health. I understand this point of view because, to some degree, I agree with it. There is a big debate in the UK going on about whether children should be given classes on mental health in school and undergo regular mental health check-ups. For his views on this, Morgan came under the wrath of the Twitterati and was abused heavily. Something he must be used to by now. Regardless, it genuinely embarrassed me to see such harsh language being used against someone giving their opinion on a universal challenge.

In these interactions on the 10th of October and in the following days there is a sense of mob mentality. It is as if we are trying to force the voices, we disagree with to be quiet or else they will be heavily abused. Mental health activism cannot be allowed to be a shouting contest where the side that shouts loudest, wins.

We need to drop the thought that there is an opposing side on this issue, because there is not. I think Morgan came under the wrath of the people on Twitter because he was not someone who is usually vocal about the subject of mental health. When he did speak about it, his opinion differed from that of the majority. Isn't the whole point of having a mental health day to encourage diverse thoughts? What use is having an annual day to talk about mental health if we drown out the voice of someone new sharing their opinions?

There is a very interesting explanation for this phenomenon. A theory from Social Psychology can explain how or why we are inherently against people who we see as different from our group. It is the Social Identity Theory (Tajfel & Turner, 1979). It can be applied to every aspect of your daily life from the friends you have to your political opinions. The Social Identity Theory transcends all levels of social organization.

The In-Group and Out-Group

Henri Tajfel, a prisoner of war in World War Two studied the phenomenon of prejudice once the war ended. He was studying in France when the persecution of Jews in Nazi Germany began, and this was how he managed to escape the atrocities. He lost many friends and family members in the holocaust. He enrolled at the French Army and was taken prisoner by the Germans. He was a Jew living among the Nazis as a prisoner, but his captors were unaware of his heritage. Once the war ended, he worked for the rehabilitation of war refugees and helped them settle in their new homes. He set his sights on the science of prejudice to understand what led to the genocide and ethnic cleansing of millions of innocent lives.

He conducted a simple experiment which displayed how little it takes for people to start differentiating themselves from others. He collected a group of 64 teenage boys in a room and showed them slides that had dots all over them on a screen. The task was to guess the number of dots on the screen. The participants had been told it was a test of their visual acuity.

Once the participants made their guesses, they were told that two groups would be formed, one for those who underestimated the number of dots and the other of those who overestimated the same. In reality, these two groups were created randomly but this fact was not revealed to the participants. The boys were then asked to assign some real money, although not much to another fellow participant. They were not told the name of the participant but were told whether they belonged to the same or the other group.

It was observed that the participants assigned more money to the members of the same group (in-group) than the people of the other group (out-group) (Tajfel, 1971). The groups had been formed very recently, on flimsy criteria. They had no relevant past or a foreseeable future. The groups had been formed on the arbitrary criteria of estimating the number of dots on a screen. Despite all these seemingly insignificant factors, the participants displayed a high degree of in-group favouritism. This study made Tajfel one of the most prominent social psychologists of the 20th century since he showed how little it takes for prejudice to form.

The in-group is the group of people we relate to. It is the group we find comfort in and where we can express ourselves. The in-group is almost always considered the morally righteous one.

The out-group is the 'other' people. It is the group that has people who either do not talk about the issue in question or differ in opinion. You can see this grouping in almost every facet of life like students studying Arts or Science or students from two universities in the same city. Most of the time, the animosity between the groups is mild and even humorous but there are issues where the out-group is seen as the source of all evil. This is most commonly seen in politics where the animosity can become so extreme that it leads to violence and subsequent death. Political rivalries regularly lead to the death of party workers and this is a scarily universal phenomenon.

Think of it as a segregation of people into us-vs-them. In extreme situations, a group starts thinking that an individual is either with them or against them. If you are with the group, you are good. You are moral. You are righteous (Dare I say patriotic?). However, if you are against the group then you are evil. You are morally bankrupt. You are a traitor.

Within the world of mental health, the out-group is seen as the people who do not talk about mental health and try to impose their own ideas on what is considered a sensitive subject. Piers Morgan was abused not because what he said was wrong, but because he does not usually talk about mental health. He was automatically put into the out-group and anything the out-group does is bad. The problem is that if we truly wish to encourage people to talk about mental health and all its aspects, we need to give them some leeway to be wrong. We need to be open to different people expressing their different opinions.

We cannot continue to abuse people if they get something wrong and if we really want them to engage in fruitful discussions. This will only alienate the people who were trying to put forth their ideas.

People are not perfect. They do not always know everything and sometimes, they are wrong. It would be better for everyone involved if we back up our claims with evidence instead of insulting the person we are arguing against. An argument is not there to be won; it is there so that all the people involved can learn.

Mental health IS NOT an us-vs-them fight. It is a united effort against mental illnesses and to extend help to people who are suffering. The objective of raising mental health awareness is that people do not feel ashamed to ask for help or to express their opinion on the same. If we keep fighting each other, there is no chance that we will make long-lasting and effective changes.

In the case of Piers Morgan, he was not wrong to propose the idea of teaching children about resilience but his idea of using the term mental strength was narrow and un-holistic. I would have been more satisfied if someone had shared this opinion with him instead of hurling insults. Another notion Morgan spoke about which brought him under fire was that people need to have a stiff upper lip when dealing with problems.

The belief in the stiff upper lip is mostly applied to men who are often told to 'toughen up' and deal with their emotional problems. Understandably, this is a major contributor to the stigma surrounding mental disorders. Morgan says that we need to drop the idea that 'everything is going to be alright' and focus on the idea that 'life is tough and here is how you should prepare for it.'

Again, both these ideas go hand in hand instead of being at odds with each other. Many times, when we face an issue in our life, we face the emotional repercussions of it. These repercussions range from mild to extreme. If a person believes that the emotional toll of the problem is so high that they cannot handle it alone, they should be encouraged to seek emotional support. It does not matter whether it comes from friends, family or a therapist as long as it is comforting. Once the emotional stress has been handled, they can tackle the problem that caused it in the first place together.

Of course, being able to solve problems alone is good but if you feel like you need support, you do not need to be ashamed to ask for it. Saying that 'everything will be alright' is a part of providing emotional support, but there is another phrase that should follow it, 'We are going to work on it.'

When Yashasvi, the 19-year-old boy who had been suffering from severe clinical depression, was recovering, he often came across many people who were in the same predicament as him. He would often be asked, "Does it get better?" He would not just say that it gets better. He would say, *"It won't get better just like that. You will have to put in a lot of work and a lot of effort into it and that is the only way things improve."*

People suffering from mental disorders have a battle going on with their own mind. It is a battle that goes on all the time with no respite. Yashasvi had admitted to often having thoughts of jumping from the balcony of the gym he went to while recovering, but he consciously told himself to not do it. When telling himself the same thing over and over got hard, he would seek emotional support but most of the time he had to do it alone.

This is another problem with mental illnesses, everyone who is outside our body is merely a support system. The fighting against our own mind has to be done individually. As I wrote in my previous book, 'The people around you willing to help can be your allies, your weapons or anything that you need them to be, but they cannot fight the battle for you. You will have to do that yourself. Every moment of every day.' Again, we see that Morgan was not suggesting something in opposition to the idea of emotional support. He was proposing something that should exist alongside it and not in place of it although, maybe, unconsciously.

Emotional Intelligence

Emotional intelligence is an idea that is only 30-years-old at the most. It was proposed by Peter Salovey, but the most influential work on it was done by Daniel Goleman who released his book *Emotional Intelligence* in 1995. The book was a major success and was loved by both academicians and the general population. I referred to it before writing this book because I wanted to understand how he managed to propose such a complex idea in a language that was easily understandable.

The concept of emotional intelligence is very simple. Since academic intelligence does not always predict success in life, there must be other factors at play. Maybe another kind of intelligence. Goleman said that emotional intelligence is the ability to sense emotions that have not been conveyed verbally and respond to them appropriately. These emotions could exist in the people around us or within us. He said that emotional intelligence has two facets. One is the action that is performed on an emotion, that is, recognising and regulating an emotion; the other is who the action is taken on, that is, whether it is taken on someone around us or the self.

The level of a person's emotional intelligence is measured by the Emotional Quotient (EQ), an idea that follows the measurement of intellectual aptitude. Since there is so much emphasis on the emotions of a person and those around them, it is surprising that the definition of mental health as used by the WHO does not include any aspects of emotional intelligence. It could be down to the fact that the concept is relatively new. Irrespective of this, any definition of mental health that does not include the emotional wellbeing of a person and society is, in my humble opinion, an incomplete one.

Resilience focuses on making sure that a problem in life is solved as soon as possible, but it does not talk about what happens when a problem persists and starts taking a psychological toll on the person. The pressure could express itself in the form of emotional turmoil like angry outbursts, pangs of sadness, extended crying or it could distort their thinking process to manifest as lower self-esteem, misanthropy, etc. A person with a higher level of emotional intelligence is less likely to stigmatize mental illness than someone with a lower level of emotional intelligence. (Armstrong, 2015)

When we look back at Yashasvi's case, he was someone who always solved his problems as quickly and efficiently as possible. When he was faced with a problem that persisted despite his best efforts, he was ashamed to ask people for help. He felt there was nothing more he could do. He believed that his life was worth nothing. What could have helped him at that point when he felt he did not have any more options? Knowledge of emotional intelligence and a little dose of hope.

Yashasvi was an introvert through most of his childhood. He had a few friends in high school. Despite this, he felt extremely attached to the people he was close to and had a sense of contentment. When his support system fell apart and he found himself isolated, he did not know how to convey the few emotions he felt to the world. The problem was that he did not know what he was feeling very well either. He would confuse sadness with anger and frustration with remorse. This was a problem with the first facet of emotional intelligence – self-awareness. Because he did not know what he felt accurately, conveying these emotions to anyone else was out of his reach.

Clinical depression also hinders our ability to understand or perceive emotions of others. Even if Yashasvi saw someone crying in front of him, he would not feels a thing. He would instead be wondering why this person was crying. This is the second facet of emotional intelligence – empathy. It is the ability to recognize the emotions of those around us. Since the young boy could not understand his emotions or those of the people around him, regulating or having an influence on either of these was a challenge in itself.

Ciarrochi and colleagues (1996) found a relationship between emotional recognition and depression. There is also some evidence of deficits in emotional recognition in depressed patients. (Downey and colleagues, 2008)

Regulating emotions of the self is something that many people struggle with across the globe. In India, unrequited love is romanticized, and it is the perfect example of an emotion which eludes self-control, the third facet of emotional intelligence. You will see poems written, movies made and stand-up comedy shows held about one-sided love, but it is very rare that you will hear someone talking about controlling it. Why don't we hear more stories about people accepting other's choices and moving on? Why is obsession encouraged and self-regulation ignored?

When we feel a very strong emotion, it is not always the best option to express it in all its extremity. Women have been stalked and killed because some men were angry with them for not returning their love. A healthier and much less violent option would be to teach people how to regulate their emotions and express them in a healthier manner. If we could accept and regulate our negative emotions, we would be a healthier society.

In the case of Yashasvi, we saw that his extreme anger led to him being isolated from most of the world. He only found comfort in social media while being a non-participant observer. He released the anger within himself when he mutilated his own body or when he attempted suicide. These were some of the emotions that dominated his mind before he went completely numb. If he had possessed some self-control, he would have found ways to express his emotions of anger or sadness to the people around him calmly. Instead, he would indulge in physical altercations. He would punch a wall or a heavy object to release his anger. This technique of emotional expression helped no one at all and only made his emotions more extreme.

The fourth facet, emotional influence is something that does not necessarily tie in with the ideas of mental health but for the sake of continuity, we will discuss it in short. Emotional influence, as the term suggests, is the ability of a person to regulate or influence the emotions of the people nearby. It is a quality that is often found in leaders and other successful people.

To summarize the concept of emotional intelligence, we will take an example. Yashasvi, who we know from before, and his friend Ruchi were supposed to meet at a restaurant at 17:00 hours. It was the first time Yashasvi was meeting someone in months, and he was nervous about it. For some reason, Ruchi had to cancel the plan at the last moment and she apologized for it multiple times. This was something that made Yashasvi feel anger and disappointment, but instead of lashing out at his friend he did the following.

He first introspected and figured out what part of the incident infuriated him the most. Because it was the first time, he had agreed to meet someone in months, he felt used when the plan fell through. This meant that it was not the cancellation of the plan that disappointed him but the meaning that the meeting carried for him that made him sorrowful (self-awareness). Then he asked Ruchi what made her cancel the plan at the last minute because he could see that she was sad through facial cues like red eyes and messy eye make-up. He could also tell that Ruchi was distracted while talking to him (empathy). He found out that her grandfather had had a heart attack and she had to rush to the hospital. Yashasvi understood this and shared how he felt angry when he read her message about the cancellation but he now understood her problems. He told her how much the meeting meant to him and this helped her understand his point of view as well (self-control). Now both of them knew what the other was feeling and why they felt these things. This opened a path for mutual interaction and improvement of feelings. He offered her a compassionate ear and talked to her till she felt better, and she did the same for him (emotional influence).

We see that a highly emotionally arousing situation was controlled through the simple use of emotional intelligence. If Yashasvi had handled this as he would have when he was depressed, things would have gone down differently. He would have probably ranted at Ruchi for abandoning him and then not talked to her for ignoring him. He would have also gone on to denigrate himself for trusting a person after so long. It would have been another few months or probably more before he agreed to meet someone again. Ruchi would have been left with the feeling of prolonged guilt. Situations where the people involved have emotional intelligence witness less drama and extreme emotions; they are the best for a meaningful conversation.

For a person who is suffering from any mental disorder, this power can come in handy since they will know themselves better and know how to express their emotions in a healthy manner. If youngsters are taught about and encouraged to improve their EQ, we would make a major move towards an emotionally-healthy society. Despite the many advantages teaching emotional intelligence has, there are some barriers that it needs to overcome.

Currently, there is a lot of emphasis put into ensuring that people do not let emotions colour their decisions. Emotions are looked down upon and no one can express their emotions lest they be judged and open themselves up to bias. There are many people who try to minimize the emotions they feel in order to be appear credible and unbiased. Experiencing fewer emotions also leads to higher objectivity and a more intellectual approach.

The problem with this outlook is that we ignore the fact that emotions are a part of human nature. Emotions are one of the many things that make us human and if we focus on wiping them out, we end up losing a part of ourselves. The aim of any social subject should not be to minimize biases, but to recognize the biases we have and how they could affect decisions.

* * *

When we talk about mental health and emotional health, there is a small, technical difference that exists between the two. Let me try and explain this concept better with an example. Consider a situation where you scored poor marks in an important exam and your teachers scolded you in front of your classmates. The low academic score and public humiliation is the stressor in our story. Your mental health will determine how you think about this stressor. Whether you think that you are a failure in life or see it as a chance to improve will indicate your mental health.

Mental health has a role in how we perceive life events. It is the difference between thinking that a low score means you are stupid or that it shows where you can improve further. Every stressor leads to an emotional reaction. Emotional health is about how accurately we label our emotions and how well we can express them. It also includes what strategies we can devise to prevent this situation from repeating. In our example, it is emotionally healthy to be aware of the fact that we feel disappointed and humiliated, and are comfortable enough to express it to someone like a good friend or a family member.

Neither mental nor emotional health means that you will never be sad or disappointed. It means that you will be able to think about the events in your life in a realistic and rational manner. It also means that you will be able to label your feelings and express them to another person in order to feel better. Emotional health can be thought of as a component of mental health, but they are not exactly the same thing.

* * *

Taking all these ideas and opinions in our understanding, let us try and create a new definition of mental health. We will use the current definition as a template.

The definition has five main parts:

- state of well-being

- individual realizes his or her own potential

- can cope with the normal stresses of life

- can work productively and fruitfully

- make a contribution to her or his community

Out of these, the state of well-being and coping with normal stresses of life are parts of resilience. We need to incorporate a sense of emotional intelligence into this definition. The main aspects of emotional intelligence, related to mental health, are self-control, self-awareness and empathy.

Mental health is defined as a state of psychological and social well-being in which every individual can cope with the normal stresses of life, can label and express their emotions accurately and can process information rationally and realistically.

This definition is simply a proposal that I believe can be used in the future as when the WHO seeks to update its definition. As mentioned earlier, the zeitgeist of the time often influences the definition used as the formal definition of mental health. Currently, there is no major on-going work on emotional intelligence but when it eventually begins, I believe that the new definition will be very close to this one.

There are many people who are making efforts to raise mental health awareness however, if we try to advocate for something, we do not fully understand we are not going to end up making any long-term changes.

Mental health is a concept that has been defined diversely over decades depending on the major psychological influence of the time and our scientific understanding of health. The definition may keep changing but it is important that we understand the concept that each definition tries to explain. Resilience and emotional intelligence are two core concepts that help us understand mental health and give us strategies to care for it.

The future of mental health care is rooted both in prevention and cure. Prevention will include building resilience in young children and improving their emotional intelligence. The aim of classes on mental health should not be to identify symptoms of a mental disorder; instead it should focus on the education and training of children so they can help a friend in distress.

It is important that, while trying to initiate a conversation on mental health, we do not end up getting caught up in a mob mentality where we drown out any unconventional thoughts by the sheer volume and intensity of protests. It is important that we encourage people to become more aware without feeding them half-truths and misinformation.

Section III

Understanding Mental Illnesses

Knowing the definition of mental health and understanding what mental illnesses are like, are two different things. While mental health is not just the absence of mental illness, it is important to understand these illnesses. Disorders of the mind are very different from those of the body.

When people hear the term 'mental illness,' they mostly focus on the 'mental' part. The mental part is related to the brain and people come to think it has something to do with the brain, but that is not completely true. Mental health is about the mind.

The mind has been conceptualized differently in different times. In India, people consider the mind as the 'soul,' the *'mann'* or the 'spirit.' The Hindi word for psychiatrist is *'Manochikitsaka,'* which translates to a doctor of the mind, not the brain.

While the mind is considered the part of the body, it doesn't fall ill the same way.

How Are Mental Illnesses Caused?

In the first section, we discussed how, in the past, people believed mental illnesses were caused by spirits and demonic possessions. Thankfully, people realized that this was not the case eventually. Now, there is a debate on whether these illnesses were caused due to the psychology or biology of the person. This debate can be understood with a simple example. In the case of Yashasvi, a psychiatrist (professing the biological perspective) would say that it was caused due to genetic predispositions to depression or a chemical imbalance in the brain. The psychologist, on the other hand, would say that it was caused by inability to manage emotions and a distorted view of reality. So, who is right?

Technically, both of them are right. And yet neither of them is correct too. Currently, the psychiatric view dominates the discourse about mental health. It is believed that mental illnesses are caused by chemical imbalance in the brain like serotonin, dopamine, etc. Despite the widespread belief among even those who encourage people talking about mental health and illnesses, there simply is not any conclusive evidence that mental disorders have a *purely* biological cause. Psychiatrists and other social workers often tell people that mental illnesses are caused by a chemical imbalance. Doing so when there is no scientific evidence or tests to confirm this raises an ethical issue (Lacasse & Leo, 2015). While there is a correlation between levels of neurotransmitters and depression patients, no causation has been established scientifically as yet.

This was also demonstrated in Yashasvi. He was on various psychotropic drugs for years, but they had little to no effect. While many will claim that it was because of an inappropriate combination of the drugs, the more likely answer is that it was because the causes of mental illnesses like depression or anxiety are not just imbalances in the brain. If this was the case, Yashasvi would have felt better within three months of being on his medicines. The psychological point of view is right in the sense that a distorted view of reality and extreme negative emotions are predecessors to mental illness, but this only proves a correlation and not a causation.

The Biopsychosocial Model

Most of the models on health care have a biomedical approach. They focus on a cause and its effects, and then create medicines or other strategies to reduce the effects (symptoms) or go right to the cause. This model works well for physical illnesses but when it comes to mental illnesses, it does not always ensure long-term solutions. The biomedical model era has been characterized by a wide lack of clinical innovation and poor mental health outcomes (Deacon, 2013). The biopsychosocial model (Engel, 1977) of mental illnesses proposes that they are not just caused by one thing but by many complex interactions.

When Yashasvi had depression, his social surroundings played a role in it. His society considered clearing a competitive exam as success and everything else as failure. This put a lot of pressure on him and made him fear failing. His friends and family were not much help either. They played a role in the development of this disease too. The lack of social support and external pressure made him have extreme emotions and low self-esteem. He had recurrent thoughts about being a failure, of suicide and self-harm. This led to an inappropriate chemical balance in his brain and his subsequent depression.

We should not only focus on fixing the hormonal imbalance in the brain. In doing so, we would be ignoring many other factors that often play a role in mental illness. This is what sets them apart from physical illnesses. A broken bone would not be affected by whether the people around want it to be fixed or not. It would not be affected by whether the person getting treatment for it has low self-esteem or thoughts of suicide. If the broken bone is treated, it will get better, simple as that.

Saying that mental illnesses happen *only* due to genetic predispositions or chemical imbalance is narrow and myopic. Disorders of the mind are more complex than that. If we want to treat them, we cannot simply focus on one aspect. We need to focus on changing the person's thought processes and the people in the surroundings. Most aspects of mental illness and psychological well-being are influenced by social factors (such as gender, social class, race and ethnicity, and household patterns). (Mechanic & McAlpine, 2002)

The model is criticized because it does not make many contributions to the doctor's clinical approach, but the fact is that it opens up the gates to many more ways that mental illnesses can be treated. The problem with it is that it shows just how hard it can be to treat mental illnesses. A psychiatrist cannot be expected to change or transform the society a person is living in. The psychiatrist also cannot change the thoughts than run through the patient's mind.

The model shows that when we are treating a mental illness, the social context and surroundings are important as well, and the community around a mentally ill person needs to change itself too. That is why most modern treatments include a team of experts instead of just a psychiatrist. The team consists of a psychiatrist, a psychologist, a social worker and a caretaker for the patient.

Social change is one of the core principles for improving mental health care and reducing the stigma attached to it.

Physical Illnesses vs. Mental Illnesses

You wouldn't tell someone with cancer to just get over it, would you? How can you say the same thing to someone with depression?

There are very few statements that could be more short-sighted or detrimental to mental health activism than this one. I can guarantee you that anyone who claims to be working for mental health awareness or knowing about it must have said this line or something similar at some point in their life. This line is not necessarily incorrect. The person saying it is trying to make you realize that mental illnesses are as real as cancer and cannot be 'gotten over' simply. The problem with this line is that it compares a mental illness to a physical illness and the only thing the two share is that they are real. Apart from this, there is little similarity between the two. Another popular comparison made is the one with a broken foot or any another limb. As we discussed briefly above, mental illnesses do not heal the same way as a physical illness. This is not the only difference between them. Let us discuss all the other ones and take the example of the oft quoted 'broken leg' along on our journey.

The clinical study of any illness has three major parts, the diagnosis: where the disease is identified; prognosis: where the disease is treated and, aetiology: where the causes of the diseases are searched for.

Aetiology

Let us first start on how these two occur (aetiology). A broken leg happens after an accident. It happens suddenly with no possible anticipation of it. No footballer goes on the football pitch expecting their leg to be broken (unless they are playing Stoke City FC), and no passenger can predict their vehicle will have an accident. In contrast to this, when it comes to a mental illness like depression or anxiety, the changes are gradual. It does not happen overnight, it happens eventually. The depression takes its time and before you know it, you have nowhere left to run.

For Yashasvi, it started with pessimism. He felt like he was not good enough and that his career had nothing exciting to offer him. This pessimism led to frustration, the pent-up frustration to sadness and this sadness ended up becoming emotional numbness. All of this happened over a span of two to three months. You will never hear about a leg breaking over the course of months.

Another aspect of aetiology is that for a broken leg, you will always know the cause and there will always be just one cause. You will not see a leg breaking because of the community it was located in or the thoughts it had. (Mostly because a leg cannot think). Social surroundings may play a role, but they do so indirectly. A person from a lower socio-economic stratum will have access to fewer nutrients and this may lead to brittle bones, which are more susceptible to breaking. The role of social factors in a physical illness is indirect at best. In a mental illness on the other hand, the causes can be many and sometimes, they can be none.

In Yashasvi's case, the best cause everyone could find was a genetic predisposition. There are many other cases where no apparent cause has been found. As we have just discussed, the causes of a mental illness are multiple, and they could be biological, psychological or social or all three combined.

Diagnosis

Diagnosing an illness is basically a mystery-solving exercise wherein we use clues and symptoms to reach a working diagnosis. The diagnosis of mental illnesses is very different from physical illnesses as well. If we show the X-ray of a fractured leg to any doctor, they would not take too long to say that the foot is broken. The problem with mental illnesses on the other hand, is that they do not always mean the same thing to different people. What is depression to me, may just be regular sadness for another, so in this case how do we say that someone has a mental disorder?

For this, psychiatrists use a tool called the Diagnostic Statistic Manual (DSM) or the International Classification of Diseases (ICD).

The goal of this tool is to ensure that if Doctor A diagnoses a patient with major depressive disorder, then Doctor B also comes to the same diagnosis when they meet the patient. This property in statistics is called the 'reliability' of a tool. The DSM is published by the American Psychological Association and the ICD is developed by the WHO.

Initially, the ICD was considered superior. The third revision to the DSM (DSM-III) in 1987, changed everything. It gave a clear description for each disorder and each symptom that needs to be looked at before diagnosing a mental illness. DSM-III changed the game and helped it overtake the previously favoured ICD. Since then, the DSM has gone through two revisions and we are currently at DSM-V. The ICD is currently in its 10th iteration and ICD-11 is expected to be published some time in 2019.

A major difference between the two is that ICD is more accessible compared to the DSM. At the National Academy of Psychologists Conference organized by my college, Ramanujan College, Delhi University, I was interested in buying the two so I could go through them and compare their organization. The ICD-10 was available for Rs. 650 (~$10) whereas the DSM-V was being sold at

Rs. 14,500 (~$210). I made the smart decision of looking for a soft copy of both online. The accessibility is the reason that most modern research uses the ICD while studying mental disorders.

The Role of the Patient

The DSM and the ICD can be thought of as a list of the normal ranges for any body fluid. Think of it in this sense, the ICD tells a psychiatrist what the normal range for haemoglobin (hypothetically) should be in a healthy individual, but how will the psychiatrist know what the level is in a patient. After all, as we discussed, there is no biological test yet that can test for mental stress. For this, the psychiatrist uses self-report inventories.

Self-report inventories involve questions where the patient is asked to introspect and answer on the basis of their own understanding of their emotions. The questions could be, "How often do you think about dying?" or "Do you feel like your life is not worth living?." It is from the answers to these questions that a psychiatrist gauges the psychological state of an individual. In the case of a physical illness, the doctor does not need to ask how bad the patient thinks the fracture is or how far along their cancer is. In psychiatry, insight from the patient is paramount.

This method of diagnosis brings about a very important line of questioning. How reliable is it? Let us take the example of a 17-year-old boy named Anmol. Anmol has been behaving different from his usual self. He is more isolated, aggressive and distracted than he was at a younger age. His family believes he is depressed. Anmol knows that he is suffering from depression because everything he has heard about what depression feels like, applies to him. He feels a void inside and has thoughts of harming himself. The problem is that he does not want to get better. He believes that he is a disgrace for being depressed and any attempt to get better will fail and bring him more shame. He does not wish to improve. Isolation is all he longs for.

One day, his parents take him to a psychiatrist and the doctor asks him many questions about what he thinks daily.

"Do you feel like a failure?" asked the doctor.

"Not at all." Anmol replied, even though he does.

He believed that his life had been full of failures. Yet, he lied about it to the doctor because he did not want to get better.

What does the psychiatrist do now?

The bitter fact is that the doctor can do nothing in this situation. Unless there is a conscious effort from the patient to get better, and unless the patient is willing to be open and honest with the doctor, there is nothing that a psychiatrist can do. The most that a psychiatrist can prescribe is a series of Electro-Convulsive therapy sessions. These are considered to be the sure-shot way to cure depression, but again, if the patient does not want to get better and insists on having a pessimistic thought cycle, the effect of ECT wears off soon.

There is another topic of discussion that may arise in your mind – who gets to decide what thinking is deviant to the point of a mental illness and what thinking is not? It again becomes a debate of psychiatrists playing social engineers trying to label behaviour that they do not like as a mental illness and the rest as the norm. This discussion is more complex than it seems as it questions the basic concept of mental illnesses as a biological truth. The whole topic could fill a whole book on its own, but if you wish to know more about it you can refer to the work of JC Wakefield (1992).

Prognosis

The next part is the treatment (prognosis) of this illness. A broken leg will be put under an X-ray machine and the tests will show a clear fracture in the images. This test will also show the degree of the fracture and the course that needs to be taken. No such test exists for a mental illness.

There is no blood test, X-ray or any other physical test that you can take which will show you that a person is mentally ill. Work in this domain has led to the development of functional MRI (fMRI) which has shown promising results but nothing concrete has been proven yet. This also leads to many people denying the existence of mental illnesses, which can be easily disproved using historical data and current research.

Once the broken leg has been covered with PoP, it does not need any more attention from the patient. The patient is a passive observer when the leg is being repaired. They do not have to make a conscious effort for the leg to get better. For mental illness, the situation is exactly the opposite. A person who is mentally ill needs to put in a conscious effort at all times to get better. It is a conscious fight against the mind and it is perennial. It goes on while the person is about to sleep, studying, playing or doing anything for that matter. The prognosis is the hardest part of every mental illness. Many people do not make it through this phase. Having to fight what your mind tells you all the time is not everyone's cup of tea. You have to second guess what your mind is telling you. This is what a mental illness leads to – losing trust in the voice inside your mind.

Can you hear that voice inside your head? The one that is reading this out for you? What if it started telling you that you are worthless? Focus on the fact that this is not a foreign voice in your head, it is your own voice, your own mind, the one that has been with you for as long as you can remember, telling you all these things. You grew up with this voice, you won hypothetical arguments in the shower with this voice and now this voice is telling you terrible things about yourself. Who are you fighting? Is it your mind or is it yourself? Is there a difference?

The next part comes about how this illness is talked about. A broken leg is sympathized with and a mental illness is looked at with sceptic eyes. It is this phase of an illness that most of our well-meaning mental health activists talk about when they make the analogy we discussed above. Since this analogy only focuses on the diagnosis and does not give any thought to their cause or treatment, I consider this popular analogy a narrow and, in the long run, a detrimental one.

Suffering from a mental illness also generates a very transient feeling of empathy and care, while a broken leg generates empathy for as long as the leg is broken. If you tell a person you have depression, chances are you will not be taken seriously in the first place. In case you are taken seriously and shown a level of empathy, this compassion will be short-lived. You will probably be rebuked if you talk to the same person again after a few months and say that mothing has changed. This is when most people hear the phrases 'get over it,' 'stop seeking attention or 'stop being lazy.' It comes a while after the diagnosis, when people expect things to magically be okay. This also comes down to the invisibility of mental illnesses. Technology has not developed to a point where we can show a person a test result and say that our illnesses are still as bad as they were before.

Despite these differences, both mental and physical illnesses are ultimately treatable. Yes, there is a high chance of relapse in mental illnesses, but it does not mean that they can never be cured. Misery, whether physical or psychological, can go away ultimately.

I hope this section has helped you understand what mental illnesses are. As you have learned, mental illnesses are very different from physical ones. They are diagnosed, treated and accepted differently. Physical illnesses may have a purely biological cause, but mental illnesses have various facets, and it is important that we treat all of them in order to have long-term benefits. This includes treating the biology, improving the thought process and sensitizing society. We do not need to change society if we were trying to treat dengue or a sprained wrist. But to treat a mental disorder long-term, we need to educate society and help them understand the seriousness of the problem. We need to do it now and we need to do it as one. The world will become a mentally-healthy place only when we are willing to progress as a united entity.

Section IV

For and against Mental Health Awareness

This subject is what made me want to write this book. Most of the books I got my hands on which talk about mental health only do so in a closed environment. They do not take the arguments and problems that some people have with mental health care and awareness into account. It seems that people find comfort in talking to a set audience and being in an echo chamber instead of keeping their minds open and reach a better understanding. In this section of the book we are going to discuss the various arguments that are raised against raising mental health awareness and the current mode of mental health care.

The Szaszian Hurdle

Thomas Szasz…has been one of the few writers who have helped keep me sane in this insane business.

– Dr. David Stein, Professor of Psychology and Criminal Justice, Virginia State University

How much liberty does a person have? Do we have absolute control of our body? If we do, then why is self-harm or suicide not accepted as a personal choice?

Thomas Szasz is a largely forgotten person in the world of psychiatry today, but in the 1960s he was one of the most popular psychiatrists in the USA. Born to a Jewish family in Budapest, his family moved to the USA in 1938 when Hungary decided to side with Nazi Germany. He was greatly despised and feared by his peers due to his constant criticism of psychiatric practices. In short, he was a musician who did not like music.

Szasz moved from Hungary to the USA with a hatred for the psychiatry practiced in the United States. He was convinced that talking and imprisonment were not legitimate practices of medicine and thus, psychiatry was not a real science.

The following short story should help you understand what his issues with psychiatry were.

Psychiatrist: So, am I insane?

Colleague: Well, since you have a delusion, evidently you are.

Psychiatrist: Oh no, there you go again! Now you say that if I have a delusion, I am insane. But you just said that I am insane. In that case, my belief is not a delusion, but a correct idea. Therefore, I have no delusion. Therefore, I am not, after all insane. It is only a delusion that I am insane; hence I have a delusion; hence I am insane; hence I am right; hence I am not insane. Isn't psychiatry a magnificent science?

Colleague: The most magnificent, my dearest colleague! But of course, it's necessary to master it as well as only you or I have.

Szasz would often make his students question the basic assumptions of psychiatric care of the mentally ill. Here is an example he quoted often. One of his students said that since a particularly female patient had been diagnosed with severe depression, she needed to be given drugs to treat the same. Szasz would then mockingly say, "You wish to 'treat' depression by using 'drugs?'"

This confused the students who had always been taught that an illness needs to be treated using drugs. He would then go to the blackboard and write down the word 'depression' in bold letters.

"What is the difference between an unhappy person and a depressed one?" He would ask authoritatively. "Isn't every person who has depression basically an unhappy one who has multiple problems in his/her life? What does the use of the term 'depressed' achieve other than making an unhappy person look like a sick one?"

Szasz was against the fundamental idea that mental illnesses were real. He believed that the things that were called mental illnesses were actually just 'problems in living.' These problems had been 'psychiatrized' by the doctors of the time. For him, illnesses of the mind were metaphorical and non-existent in a physical sense. He fought against the founder of psychiatry, Benjamin Rush.

Rush hypothesized that since the mind is just another part of the body, it must be governed by the same laws, get ill in the same way and be treated identically as well. Szasz argued only a visible cellular pathology should be considered an illness. The cell is the basic unit of life and Szasz believed that if a body is sick then the cell must be sick as well, or at least, there must be some observable change in their physiology. The problem with this definition is that it excludes illnesses like migraines as well. The migraine was a widely-accepted illness in the 1960s, but Szasz did not have any words against it.

Another rebuttal of this argument was that Szasz's belief excluded infectious diseases as well since they did not offer an observable cellular change before the advent of the discipline of microbiology. Let me explain further.

Before we knew that illnesses like Diphtheria or Measles were caused by tiny microorganisms, Szasz would have said these illnesses were not real since they did not cause any cellular pathological changes. This idea would have obviously been laughed off at the time. Moreover, many mental illnesses have now been found to have a genetic factor. Since the genes are carried in the DNA of each cell, we now have a cellular pathology of mental illnesses at a molecular level. So, even if we go by Szasz's very narrow definition, mental illnesses now are 'real' illnesses. Then what is the difference between a neurological disorder and a mental disorder?

Psychiatrists and psychologists alike have come to the conclusion that most mental illnesses have a basis in the brain and that they are 'brain diseases,' but that it is not necessarily the end of mental illnesses.

This argument brings about a debate on where we draw the line between neurology and psychology is. Currently, neurology is considered the study of the brain (the hardware) and psychology is seen as the study of the mind (the software). Although all humans may have the same brain at a gross anatomical level, the connections between the neurons change over time. These changes are heavily influenced by the environment one lives in. Hence, each brain is different at the microscopic neuron level (Barrett, 2009). If Barrett's reasoning is accepted then it is unnecessary for neurology to be the future destination of psychology, where the two disciplines are combined.

Chemistry and Physics are known to be interlinked, but there has been no amalgamation of the two over centuries. In the same way, neurology and psychology are expected to continue as two separate but interlinked disciplines.

Szasz also argued that every physical illness has a universal norm and any deviation from that norm is sign of an illness. Since the norms of mental illnesses are affected by ethnicity and culture, it was not a discipline that needed to be studied by scientists. We discussed this idea earlier while defining mental health as well. Psychiatrists rebutted this argument by saying that the norm a person was compared to should not derived from the population, but from the individual's past behaviour.

Szasz was also strongly against the *pathologization* of everyday life. What is the line between an individual's suffering and a pathological mental phenomenon? He believed that if we classified every personality quirk as a disorder or an illness, we would enter a new age where drugs and psychiatric labels would be the norm, and not having any illness would be looked down upon. An age where being normal is abnormal. Lowering the threshold for psychiatric diagnoses would lead to an undue increase in the number of persons labelled in such a way. (Francis, 2013)

This argument of his finds support in the fact that the diagnostic threshold for many mental illnesses has been constantly falling for multiple revisions of the DSM. It is also supported by people who are against raising mental health awareness.

One the most damning and controversial arguments made by Szasz was where he compared a psychiatrist to an astrologer. He believed that problems in everyday life did not need medical intervention. To him, if a psychiatrist promises his patient that his ills and troubles will go away with some drugs then they are no different from an astrologer who says that troubles are caused due to an unfortunate alignment of celestial bodies.

At the time, mental illnesses were only treated for biological causes but now that we have an understanding of the biopsychosocial model of mental illnesses, we can say that a psychiatrist is not the same as an astrologer. Although, at the same time, it is important that we understand that a psychiatrist alone cannot treat all mental illnesses. There are many other agents in our daily life like our family, friends, social group, etc. who play a major role in treating a mental illness.

Szasz was also one of the strongest critics of hospitalization of the mentally ill without their consent. He believed that psychiatry cannot include the imprisonment of patients. His belief that psychiatric care must be a consensual act stands strong to this day. In his time, people were sent to hospitals where they were imprisoned while they underwent treatment. Szasz said that in this position, a psychiatrist was not a doctor but a warden and the patient, a prisoner. Barring extreme cases where a mentally ill person is considered unfit to take decisions for themselves, this point is one of the most basic ideas of the human rights of the mentally ill today.

In my previous book, *The A-Z of Mental Health,* I dedicated a chapter on how the consent to treatment is one of the cornerstones of mental health care. If a doctor does not have the consent of the patient, any measures taken to improve their situation would be futile. The Mental Health Care Act, 2017 in India also took the step of describing in detail, the rights a mentally ill individual enjoys. It included the right to direct their own treatment and if a situation arises where they are unable to do so due to a lack of decision-making abilities, they can choose an advanced directive. The advanced directive is a living will.

The long detailing of the rights of the mentally ill is in stark contrast to the old act it replaced, Mental Health Care Act, 1987 which had one solitary line for the rights of the mentally ill.

Szasz was not necessarily against the profession of psychiatry. Instead he focused on making it more effective. It is said that scepticism is the first step to improvement. The sad news is that despite all his efforts, Szasz is a comparatively unknown figure in the world of psychiatry.

In western countries, the idea he fought so hard against prevails and any criticism of the same is either ignored, disdained or laughed at. He is now compared to a flat-earther fighting against the idea of a spherical Earth which in my honest opinion, is unfair to the man. He was fully dedicated to protecting civil liberty and freedom. He spent his whole life arguing against the intrusion of the doctor in the life of an individual. He believed that a person trying to die by suicide should not be stopped. "What gives us the right to save someone who doesn't want to be saved?" He would say. Self-harm was not that big a problem for him since it didn't harm anyone else. The only person it hurt was the one who did it and personal liberty is supreme, after all. Despite these, he was not against the use of voluntary psychotherapy. At a seminar in 2007, he said, "Psychotherapy is one of the most worthwhile things in the world."

The most impressive tribute to Szasz's work came in 1989 when an ailing Karl Menninger, the long-time leader of the American Psychiatry Association and someone Szasz had been fighting against all his professional life, wrote to Szasz,

I am holding your new book, Insanity: The Idea and Its Consequences, in my hands. I read part of it yesterday and I have also read reviews of it. I think I know what it says but I did enjoy hearing it said again. I think

I understand better what has disturbed you these years and, in fact, it disturbs me, too, now. We don't like the situation that prevails whereby a fellow human being is put aside, outcast as it were, ignored, labelled and said to be 'sick in his mind'.

Szasz spent his whole career working on the human rights of the mentally ill. He always kept psychiatrists on their toes. It was in his tribunals that psychiatry was exposed as a profession that abused human rights. He won over 50 awards in his lifetime and wrote hundreds of books and scholarly papers.

On 8th September 2012, Thomas Szasz died by a fall, there are many reports that allege it was a death by suicide.

His death, like his legacy, is shrouded in uncertainty.

A 'Pathetic' Existence

There are few other organized forms of criticism against existing mental health care or awareness campaigns. Most of them are written in older times from which the situation and the society has moved on. Most of the criticism I can find today are from bloggers. The most vocal or extreme of these voices I could find was that of Brendan O'Neill, a writer for The Sun and Spectator, both English newspapers.

In an article titled 'You Are Not Mentally Ill' published on April 20, 2017, O'Neill called out many things about campaigning for mental health awareness. He started by saying that there is no real taboo about mental health today. Everywhere he looks, he can see people talking about mental health and claiming to be mentally ill. He considered this labelling of being mentally ill a fashion accessory. People actually ended up telling a psychiatrist that they *want* to be bipolar.

He strongly criticized the efforts taken up by Princes Harry and William who organized a talk where people could talk about their mental health. He repeated the Szaszian idea that raising mental health awareness could lead to a situation where we diagnose daily life and every personality quirk or up and down in life is termed a disorder.

Much like Piers Morgan, he also advocated promoting resilience among people and used the example of the stiff upper lip. He repeated Morgan's ideas regarding how we should work to make people believe that they have the resources to cope with a problem instead of telling them everything will be alright.

The points I have listed here are a very watered-down form and his words were much harsher to say the least. Let us look at these points one by one. O'Neill's exact words were the following,

...how come I can't open a newspaper or flick through my TV channels or browse social media without seeing someone go into grisly depth, often replete with sad selfies, about his latest bout of mental darkness.

I think Brendan's beliefs here can be simply explained by the availability heuristic.

Heuristics are logical shortcuts or rules-of-thumb that people use in everyday life to process information quicker. These heuristics include the availability heuristic, representativeness, anchoring and adjustment among others. The availability heuristic occurs when we see a piece of information so often that we accept it as the truth. A person is said to employ the availability heuristic whenever he estimates the frequency or probability by the ease with which instances or associations can be brought to mind. (Tversky & Kahneman, 1973). A common example is people who are afraid of flying in airplanes.

The extensive coverage given to an air-crash may make us think that it is more frequent than it is. Of course, we cannot expect the news to also tell us about the thousands of flights that land safely daily. The coverage of one plane crash may fill us with an irrational fear of flying.

In the case of Brendan O'Neill, the fact that he was surrounded by news of mental health episodes, tragedies or emotional turmoil, led him to conclude that people are comfortable with talking about their mental health or emotive state. This inference suffers from one drawback – the availability heuristic. He applied the availability heuristic when he saw so many instances of people talking about their mental health, he considered it the norm instead of a taboo as it is proclaimed. The principle of selective attention, wherein we only seek the evidence we are looking for may have also applied.

Brendan also said that he sees people share sad selfies which makes him think it is a 'replete into mental darkness.' A sentence that equates depression with sadness. This is not necessarily completely Brendan's fault. Today, the term depression has been so watered down that people confuse it with sadness. This causes the people who have been diagnosed with depression to stay silent for longer lest they be accused of trying to fit in.

His second point, that mental illnesses are now seen as fashionable or desirable is also down to the coverage that is given to mental illnesses in mainstream media. Whenever a media house covers a story of depression or suicidal tendencies, the main focus is on the recovery as a means to inspire people. What we fail to see, very often, is the dark side of mental illnesses. There is not enough discussion about how scary having a mental illness is. It does not mention the isolation that comes along with it, the self-hatred, disdain for existence and a loathing of one's own mind. You will not find any media house stress on these things when covering mental illnesses. This ignorance of harsh realities is what makes people think they are desirable. It tends to glorify the victim and ignores the brutalities they have had to face at the hands of their own mind.

People only see the attention being given to the sufferers and the interviews they get to give. They do not get to see an iota of what they have come through to be strong enough to give these interviews.

There is a shared belief that going through a mental illness makes people resilient or courageous. Yashasvi, the boy we have been talking about, was asked what his depression gave him. The researcher was expecting him to say something that was positive and optimistic. His real answer was exactly the opposite,

My depression gave me emotional numbness and pain. It made me hate my existence and it made me want to die. It made me lose my friends and isolated me for years. It derailed my professional career and left me in

a limbo, professionally, psychologically and emotionally. It took away two years of my life that I am never going to get back, and it left scars on my body that won't heal no matter how much I try.

Almost reading the person's mind, he continued,

I know you thought I would say that it made me a better human being or braver or something like that. The fact is that it did not. I may be brave, and I may be courageous not because of my depression…but despite it.

His answer is something that more people need to hear. There is a brutal honesty in his words that you will not find in many others. It tells us about the horrors of mental illness and why it is not something that people should desire. There is nothing to be gained from being mentally ill. It is nothing beautiful or loveable. It is horrible, despicable and destructive. It harms people, destroys lives and very often ends them. Mental illnesses are not beautiful or desirable. They are straight up murderous.

The latest people who have set out to 'break the taboo' on talking about mental illness – the worst enforced taboo in history! – are Princes William and Harry. As part of their Heads Together campaign, they want to shatter the stigma around mental health (lads, there's no stigma) by getting people, especially younger people, to open up about their mental travails. This week William even did a FaceTime chat with Lady Gaga to raise awareness about mental ill-health. Under the hashtag #OKtoSay, tweeters are being encouraged to gab about their ups and downs. It's time to trade the 'stiff upper lip' for a wobbly lip, stoicism for confessed vulnerability, said William this week.

Brendan touched upon a very amusing topic when he raised this point. Although, I do not think it was his intention, he ended up raising the question, "What does 'talking' about mental health mean?" It has become the tagline of almost everyone working to create mental health awareness. Everyone wishes to start a conversation about mental health but what would that conversation include?

Person A: We really need to start talking about mental health. It is such an important topic in today's times.

Person B: Indeed. We need to have a conversation about mental health. We should encourage people to talk about mental health.

Person A: Yes, let's talk about mental health.

Person B: Mental health, indeed.

Saying 'mental health' repeatedly does not start a conversation on the same.

Mental health is a concept that encompasses stress, resilience and emotional intelligence. A discussion on mental health does not have to involve talking about depression or schizophrenia, it involves helping people understand and express their emotions. Yes, there will be many people who will share the ups and downs in their lives, but we need to make sure that they also understand the difference between a professional diagnosis and a personal assumption.

I understand that this may seem harsh but if we really want people to understand the plight of the mentally ill, we need to help them understand the severity of it as well. Once we understand the severity of an individual's illness, we need to play a role in helping them recover. Just understanding someone's problems is not enough. We need to be prepared to intervene too.

I was at an event where people were talking about mental health. I like to visit them because I get an understanding of what people think and how these events are organized. There I saw a young man, around 18-years-old, talk about how he was struggling with depression. He had come all the way from the other side of the city just to share this with people. It felt great that he was comfortable sharing it at this event. I was also worried about why he had to travel so far to express his emotions; it was the first time that he had told anyone about it. He was applauded and accepted by the crowd after he got down from the stage.

What happened after that worried me.

There were people applauding his bravery, calling him courageous and inviting him for future events. But most importantly, no one was offering him any help. I did not see one person go to him and say,

"How are you feeling now?"

"Is there something I can do to help?"

Or anything remotely similar to an actual act of support. While concluding the presenters said that it was brave of him to come forward, but I was just thinking that coming forward with your problems does not end them. Tackling them does. Not one person in that hall of around 70 people helped him tackle his problems. It was like they were okay being witnesses to his fight with his mind instead of standing next to him, assisting him.

It is important that when we ask people to talk about their mental health struggles in life, we offer them help to overcome those struggles. These two go hand in hand. In a society where talking about your emotions is looked down upon, once someone has expressed their emotions, the negative ones, the next step should be to think of strategies to manage or remove them.

In India, there is a lot of stigma attached to men and their emotions. This is also seen globally. Men are four times more likely to die by suicide than women and this is mostly because of the 'hard-shell' image that is a stereotype for men.

"Mard ko dard nahi hota." (Men feel no pain). A famous dialogue by Amitabh Bachchan is often quoted whenever a guy is crying irrespective of his age. It is this issue that we are talking about when we say we wish to talk about mental health. We wish to talk about the restrictions that have been put on expressing emotions and the shame attached to feeling them. We wish to talk about the management of emotions

instead of suppressing them. We wish to talk about generating hope intrinsically instead of imbibing fear externally.

O'Neill's point about diagnosing everyday life is a valid one as we discussed in Thomas Szasz's case. The objective of tools used in the diagnosis should be to make the difference between a mentally ill individual and a healthy individual clear. The problem arises when a tool is used to create as many diagnosable people as possible. For example, the fifth revision of the DSM by the American Psychological Association includes sub-disorders that can be considered as halfway between being normal and having a disorder. Why does this category need to exist? How does it help anyone involved? It only increases the number of people on or recommended to use psychotropic drugs. Although, there is nothing wrong with most of these drugs, why do so many people need to be on them? It is as if Szasz's predictions are coming true. I must also emphasize the fact that this phenomenon is mostly centred in the USA and not in other countries.

There was one Brendan's lines that got me as close to being angry as an online blog can. In the last paragraph, his lines were,

The problem here is that people are being told it's cool not to be able to cope, to embrace the identity of fragility. They are invited to think of themselves as incapable, to build their personality around being pathetic.

The reluctant optimist in me would like to believe that his use of the term 'pathetic' was borne as a result of a flow of emotions rather than rational thought. I agree with the idea that we should encourage people to use resources at hand or increase them, but if they cannot cope with something, does that make them pathetic? Pathetic at what exactly? Pathetic at coping with life? Pathetic at fighting with the mind when it tells you every second to harm yourself? If so, then is Brendan O'Neill, the great rationalist that he is, arguing that there are people who are glad to be pathetic? Is he saying that a mentally ill person wakes up every morning thinking, *"Alright, I get to live another day of my beautiful pathetic existence and isn't that the dream!"*

No person who is mentally ill is in this condition through their own choice. If they could choose, they would choose being able to cope with their problems every time, but they cannot. It should not be a topic of shame for them to ask for help. It should not be 'pathetic' to ask for help. Maybe one of our emotional intelligence classes on empathy could help Brendan understand this concept better.

A prominent thing I observed in the work of Szasz and O'Neill is that they took up extreme positions. I do not know if these positions were chosen through free will or a desire to shock the reader. Szasz's call that psychiatrists are no different from astrologers and O'Neill's declaration that 'I can cope with life' is taboo today were extreme positions that are hardly based on any truth. The most common reason I see behind people taking such extreme positions is that it brings a lot of attention at a brisk pace.

Szasz ended up becoming the most prominent psychiatrist in the USA in the same decade as the release of his book. O'Neill has created a huge following for himself on social media, especially on British politics. The extremes bring with them a shock value and extreme criticism. The position can later be changed or apologized for, but it always puts you in the limelight. The problem with talking on extremes is that soon, the attention starts to dissipate. You end up getting a loyal following, you get a huge audience, but you end up staying away from the truth.

Another reason we see a rise in people taking extreme positions is because of the all-or-none language in use these days. In 2018, you cannot just like a thing. You must love it more than your life. You must be willing to kill for it or as the common slang goes 'die for it.' The same is true for disliking something as well. You cannot just disagree with anyone anymore, you have to hate them from the bottom of your heart, you must hate them, their family and their ancestors to be taken seriously and you must also disagree with every other opinion they have for all of eternity. We live in an age of extremes. We create them where they do not exist, and we accentuate them when they are insignificant. The truth suffers. It gets lost in this 'war' of extremes.

In those times, the Indian slogan '*Satyamev Jayate*' brings hope. 'Only truth prevails' it says, but it does not mention that truth does not prevail on its own. The truth demands work.

I am writing this book, not to shock you or grab your attention, but to bring you the reality on a subject that I hold very close to my heart. There might be many other books on it which will grab more attention and generate more debate but at the time of my writing this, I do not see any of these things around me.

I only see people talking about mental health through fiction or personal stories. I do not see people addressing the subject head on. It is tip-toed around, hinted at as a sub-theme in books but never directly tackled and that is what I am trying to change.

An Unecessary Romance

Suicidal people are just angels that want to go back home.

I like angels so much that I want to become one.

In a strange way, I had fallen in love with my depression.

You can see quotes or images with these words on social media websites. This majorly includes posts or quotes that make depression seem desirable and something that is "tragically beautiful." This is mostly seen on Tumblr or Reddit and what is going on here is, let's just say, dangerous. Mental illness is slowly being seen as a quality to be sympathized with and, in drastic cases, to be coveted. (Yu, 2018)

When people decide to discuss their problems on social media, they receive many kinds of responses. Some of these responses would be of compassion and support, some blunt and seemingly harsh, and then there is the third category of no actual responses but of likes and shares. There will be no comments of support or mild scolding, but it would only be likes, hearts and shares.

Now imagine that you posted something asking for help and you got very few responses, but when you shared your scars or cuts from self-harm, you got loads of shares and likes. Ask yourself one question, which one of these posts are you going to share again? Will it be something that might have helped but did not get any responses, or will it be you harming yourself?

Sites that allow anonymous posting end up becoming group therapy sessions with no therapist to take charge. You find people suffering like you are, but it is highly likely that instead of improving your situation, it will end up becoming a constant, painful cycle of reinforcement. This leads to people expressing their emotions and hardships, which end up looking like they are romanticizing depression.

The person is not aware that they are romanticizing something. They are sharing what they feel or think. Hence, it is important to deal with this situation sensitively. When I started researching this issue on the internet, I came across many articles that illustrated how romanticizing mental illnesses is bad. Something that all of them missed however, is the fact that people who do it are not aware of it themselves. They are not doing it on purpose. Ask anyone if they have romanticized mental illnesses and they would say no. Their actions may say otherwise. When people say things like,

"Suicidal people are angels that want to go back home."

We see this as something that is uneasy romanticism, but the people who write and share this see it as something completely different. If you tell people or shout at them to not romanticize mental illnesses, you are more likely to alienate and isolate them. It needs to be a compassionate and sensitive discussion to bear any fruit. Again, this is not an 'us versus them' fight. We do not make a difference by silencing people, but we achieve this by taking them along with us on the road to recovery. Long rants, shouting or ignoring them are not viable solutions. Discussing, reaching out and being calm are.

The next time you feel someone is romanticizing mental illnesses, do not ignore them, rant at them or scold them. Talk to them. Talk to them at a time when they are comfortable and then reach out. Do this calmly, yet assertively. Those people need help. It is up to us to at least try our best with them.

Through all these arguments we can see that there is no real argument that says we should not raise mental health awareness. People only say we should not do so because there is a chance that while de-stigmatizing something, we could end up making it look desirable.

This kind of criticism is important because it keeps us in check. They make sure that our enthusiasm to increase the reach of mental healthcare does not put us in a position where being normal is looked down upon, and where every life struggle is an illness.

Criticism is not something that anyone should be afraid of. If a critique is honest and backed up by evidence, then it must be given some thought. The fight is between general society and these disorders of the mind. The only differences we have are where we draw the lines of these disorders and the way they should be treated.

We are all in this together, and we are going to overcome these problems together as well.

Just Another Movement?

Is mental health awareness really necessary? I mean, is it really THAT important?

At any point, the world is plagued by thousands of issues. There are people working for all these issues. For everyone, their own issue is the most important one. A feminist would say that the need for social and legal equality needs immediate attention for humanity to progress. In the eyes of an environmentalist, the issue of climate change is the one that needs the greatest efforts to ensure our very survival. One person can focus on rampant corruption and another can take on human trafficking. In all these discussions, where does the issue of mental health find its place?

Before we start talking about taking the mental health movement mainstream, we need to work on making it a significant member of the health movement. The WHO (2018) released a list of the biggest threats to human health. Diseases like dengue, HIV/AIDS and the anti-vaccination movement that is mushrooming in various parts of the western world were on the list. Interestingly, there was no mention of mental health or suicide prevention. The WHO has been focussing a lot on mental health in recent years and hence, it was a surprise that it did not make it to the list.

I am going to present the argument that mental health awareness is important in two aspects. One will speak to the human in you and the other will speak to the businessman. First, let us go with the less conventional, economic reason to work towards a mentally healthy society.

Whenever an individual is suffering from a disease, whether physical or mental, their productivity and efficiency is affected. This hampers their overall output and leads to a loss for the organization they work for. On an individual level, the travel to the hospital, the appointment and the subsequent treatment, all come at a cost. Mental illness affects almost all areas of day-to-day functioning, resulting in greater disability and an increased burden on caregivers. (Swain & Behura, 2016)

Now, there are three major ways that are used to calculate the cost of a disorder, this cost is also known as the 'burden' of the particular disease. (World Economic Forum, 2011)

The most popular method is the Disability Adjusted Life Years (DALY) method, which calculates lost economic growth due to mental disorders. The idea is that the costs of any disease can be calculated in the form of the labour, the individual's loss in productivity and the capital, the expenditure on travel costs, treatment costs, etc. The loss in capital is easy to calculate since the transactions occur in the form of actual currency, but calculating the loss in labour is a challenge. To solve this, first the GDP of a defined population is calculated if no deaths occurred due to a disease. This GDP is then compared the actual GDP and we get a figure that gives us an estimate of the losses faced due to mental disorders. This figure is converted into years, which are known as Disability Adjusted Life Years (DALYs). The same method is used by the WHO as well.

According to this method, between 2015–2030, the burden of mental disorders will be USD$ 16.3 trillion. This is comparable to the burden of cardiovascular diseases and higher than that of cancer and diabetes. India alone stands to lose USD$1.03 trillion before 2030 due to mental health conditions (Bloom et al., 2014). For comparison, the estimated burden of HIV/AIDS is at USD$ 26 billion per year.

Numbers tend to lose their meaning as the number of zeroes increases. We do not really appreciate the large difference between a million, a billion and a trillion. To showcase this difference, assume that each dollar is equal to one second of time.

If you went back one million seconds, you would go 11 days into the past. If you went back a billion seconds, you would find yourself 31 years in the past. A time when the internet did not exist. If you go back one trillion seconds into the past, you will find yourself almost 32,000 years away from the present. A time when the first humans were setting foot in the Americas and a time when mammoths walked the earth. Go 16.3 trillion seconds into the past and you are 512,000 years away from current civilization. A time when *homo sapiens* had not walked the Earth!

Another way of calculating the burden of mental disorders is the human capital costs. It adds the direct and indirect costs of an illness using the available statistics and records of a small sample of the population. This method estimates a loss of USD$ 2.5 trillion in 2010, which will double by 2030. The peculiar thing is that in mental disorders, the indirect costs are higher compared to direct costs. This phenomenon is reversed in the case of most other illnesses like cardiovascular diseases and diabetes.

The last method of calculating the burden is the Value of Statistical Life (VSL) mode.

It can be understood with an example. Imagine in a population, the chances of dying due to a depressive disorder are 15 per 1,000. If some remedial measures can bring it down to 5 per 1,000 for a cost of $50,000, the VSL will be calculated as follows,

$50,000/(15–5)/1,000 = \$5,000,000.$ (Trautmann, Rehm & Wittchen, 2016)

Using this method, the burden of mental disorders is USD$ 8.5 trillion.

This helps visualize the fact that mental disorders cost a lot. To people who need to have a monetary incentive for any activity, this is it.

Do not raise mental health awareness just because it is kind, do it because it is the economical thing to do.

The other reason we need a united movement for mental health awareness is the fact that it affects almost 1.1 billion people across the world. Twenty-five percent of the human population suffers from a mental disorder at some point of their life. Thirty-six million people are suffering from AIDS globally, and the fact that there are successful campaigns running in almost every part of the world about HIV gives me hope that the same can happen for mental disorders as well. I am comparing the burden and prevalence of mental disorders with other diseases to convince you that the treatment of mental disorders and raising awareness about them must be the top-most priority for any progressive society. I do not wish to put other health movements down. I wish to give you some context on how far-reaching and deadly mental disorders are.

How does raising mental health awareness help anyone?

Would it contribute to the recovery of those who are already ill? If not, what is the point of the whole exercise? The answer is that it helps everyone, from those who are sick, to those who might be and those who are not.

A society that is well informed on mental health will stigmatize victims less. This will encourage them to seek help for their ills and speed up the recovery process. Those who might be at risk of being mentally ill, due to genetic predispositions, will be better prepared should the illness manifest at some point in their lives. Mental health awareness will help people recognize that help for psychological problems is available.

Later in the book, we are going to discuss how important community interventions are when treating a mental illness. For those community interventions to work, we need a well-educated and informed society.

Mental health needs immediate attention. We cannot let it be something we merely sympathize with but something we are proactive towards. While doing so, we also need to be careful. Making mental illnesses appear 'cool' or desirable is not something our generation can afford. These illnesses cost trillions of dollars and they never affect just one person. A person's entire social group is affected by these disorders.

A mental illness may manifest in an individual, but it affects a community as a whole.

Providing for and supporting good mental health is a public health issue like assuring the quality of drinking water or preventing and managing infectious diseases. Communities prosper when the mental health needs of its members are met. (SAMHSA, 2013)

Modern treatments of these disorders are giving positive results at levels that have never been recorded before. It is time we start using the technology and knowledge at hand to minimize the risks of mental illnesses. Finally, informed discussion about mental health on a meaningful platform is also key.

Section V

Stigma: A Silent Weapon

I see depression as a first world problem. There is no data that supports the fact that it happens to the poor. Have you ever heard of a poor person claiming to be depressed?

These were the words of one of the teachers at my college. I was leaving the college after a talk that we had organized on depression. Some people from an NGO had come to give a short presentation on myths surrounding depression. Some of them even shared their stories about battling depression and/or anxiety. On the way out, I ran in to this teacher. Let us call him Professor T.

Prof. T was pretty firm in his beliefs that mental illnesses and depression were not something that existed in poor people. Initially, I did not think he was being serious. My impression of him considered him one of the brightest minds in the college.

He was an outspoken activist for gender equality and gave mesmerizing speeches on the issues that he strongly believed in. Once reality set in, I was straightforward with him and told him that his beliefs were wrong. He asked me if I had any scientific data give to support my arguments.

Since I do not carry supporting research in my college bag daily, I could not give him any concrete evidence. I did tell him that research has shown that those suffering from poverty are significantly more likely to suffer from depressive disorders. The heartening thing to see was that he was open to being proven wrong and had an open mind throughout the conversation. Having a debate or even a discussion with anyone who has an open mind and is open to criticism, is a pleasure everyone must experience in their life.

Ideally, it should be the norm, but we do not live in an ideal world.

The discussion moved on to how depression diagnoses have increased since the 1960s when anti-depressants were first formulated. He said that he does not buy into clinical psychologists' claims that they alone can treat depression and I agreed with him on this. I said that it is insincere for anyone to claim that they *alone* can treat an illness like depression. Despite this, I re-affirm my opinion that we should not be afraid of visiting a psychiatrist. It is like a visit to any other doctor.

This conversation taught me a lot about the disparities that exist in how mental health is seen around the world. In the west, it is believed that there are too many diagnoses of mental illnesses to the point that everyday life struggles are being diagnosed as illnesses. There it is believed that we do not need to raise mental health awareness because there is already enough of it and any more would be detrimental. This was evident in the arguments made by Brendan O'Neill and Thomas Szasz.

In India and other eastern countries, the belief is that mental illnesses are primarily a luxurious problem that only the rich can afford. Here, it is believed that we do not need to raise mental health awareness simply because it does not apply to enough people. Hence, it becomes a challenge to devise a global strategy to improve mental healthcare. We can counter this problem by first focusing on the one obstacle that exists globally – stigma.

Fighting the Stigma

Stigma is a concept that has evaded a scientific definition (Goffman, 1963). Instead of exploring the scientific understanding, we will give stigma a simple dictionary definition – a mark of disgrace being attached to an individual, group or population. It has ended up becoming a sort of bogeyman for the people working to create mental health awareness.

At the Mental Health Festival 2018, arranged by the people at Mental Health Foundation of India, I talked to some volunteers about what they believed were the biggest challenges in making a mentally-healthy society. Most volunteers agreed that it was the stigma attached to visiting a psychiatrist or the fear of being labelled 'crazy.' Now we know that stigma exists in today's world, the next step, after recognizing its existence, is to understand how it works. Afterall, we need to understand something if we intend to change it. The stigma of mental illnesses works on two levels. One is the social level where people around us enforce a stigma on the person suffering and then there is the self-stigma that is imposed by the sufferer on themselves.

Some people claim that the stigma no longer exists because of how openly people are discussing mental health. They need to know that what they are seeing is a bubble of convenience and not the present reality. Yes, things are changing but it is far from being a world where people do not feel ashamed to ask for emotional support.

To understand how the stigma works, Link and colleagues (1987) carried out a very simple yet effective experiment. They proposed a hypothetical situation where the participants had two situations. One was where a former back pain patient was moving into the neighbourhood and in the other, it was a former mental illness patient.

People were asked about how they would behave with these people in general. It also included how much distance they would like to maintain with these two hypothetical people.

For the man who was a former back pain patient, people were willing to have a close relationship with him provided his behaviour and beliefs matched their own. When it came to the person with a mental illness, the participants displayed a tendency to maintain some social distance from them. Distance is not always maintained physically. Social distance is the distance we maintain with people from different social circles. The social distance between close friends is very low compared to general acquaintances.

This tendency was due to the belief that those who have a mental illness are unstable and dangerous. This distance was maintained even if the beliefs and behaviours of the two people were the same.

In general, humans unconsciously differentiate people on the basis of arbitrary differences. These differences could be as small as having a different-coloured car or wearing a different shade of jeans but what does not happen with these differences is the labelling. We do not call people who drive a black car...anything. We do not think this difference is significant enough to merit a separate label.

When it comes to differences in skin colour, language or heritage, we have labels ready quicker than a label maker. These differences are considered socially relevant but who decides what is socially relevant or not? This question is answered by the different times we live in. In the past, some cultures placed a lot of importance on crossed-eyes and equated them to having a higher intellectual capacity. Differences among people have always existed. The problem begins when negative stereotypes affect our behaviour with others. The problem begins when we let our preconceived notions get the better of our compassion. The problem begins when stigma becomes a silent weapon against the mentally ill.

'Those' People

What do Shah Rukh Khan, James McAvoy, Vidya Balan, Bradley Cooper and Salman Khan have in common?

In an analysis of movies which depicted people having a mental illness, Taylor & Dear (1980) found three major types of portrayals. The first kind was where the mentally ill person was shown as being unstable or dangerous for example, Vidya Balan's portrayal in '*Bhool Bhulaiya*' or James McAvoy's character in 'Split.' The second kind is where patients have been shown as irresponsible people who do not know how to lead normal lives and hence, need an authoritarian upbringing like Salman Khan in '*Tere Naam*' or Shah Rukh Khan in 'Devdas.' The third one is the depiction of the mentally ill as child-like individuals who have not developed at the speed they should have and hence, need special care.

The media has been a major source in the propagation of these stereotypes. In the USA, it seems like every mass shooting is done by a mentally ill person. The problem with this kind of media coverage is that it rarely talks about the kind of mental illness the shooter was suffering from. The headlines always say, "Shooter was mentally ill" along with some other words to decorate the headline.

This only perpetuates the idea that anyone who has a mental illness is dangerous and violent. The fact is that all mental illnesses do not result in violence. There are only some disorders which have been found to be a close predictor of violence (Swartz, 1998). The sooner the media houses accept this fact the better it will be for everyone.

Another problem with stigma is that it is not always overt. Sometimes, we use subtle words or linguistic variations that display our unconscious stigma against the mentally ill. Let us take the example of a person with cancer and a person with bipolar disorder. If we know someone who has been diagnosed with cancer, we say that he/she has cancer, but when someone we know is diagnosed with bipolar disorder, we say that the person 'is bipolar.' There is a small but significant difference between the two sentences.

Saying that someone has cancer indicates that the cancer is a part of their physical being, whereas saying someone is bipolar builds their identity around their mental illness.

It is also because of the formation of an unconscious in-group and out-group that this phenomenon takes place. Cancer is something that one of 'us' suffers from, but it does not lead to them being labelled 'canceric.' On the other hand, a diagnosis of schizophrenia or bipolar disorder makes the person schizophrenic and bipolar, respectively. Why does this happen?

This happens because of two reasons. One is that we see the mentally ill as an out-group or as 'those' people. 'Those' people do not need our attention and we try to maintain a social distance from 'them.' We believe 'they' are dangerous. 'They' are unstable, which is why if we obtain a single fact about them, we form their (everyone with a mental illness) whole identity based on it. Incumbents are thought to "be" the thing they are labelled. (Estroff, 1989)

Another reason is that we see mental illnesses as something under the control of the patient. It is the belief that those who are living with depression are doing so, of their own choice and that their illness is in their control. This belief is widespread. An example that you might be able to relate to is that of drug addiction.

There is a widespread belief that if a drug addict wanted to get sober, he/she would manage to do it. We believe that their addiction is in their control and they can stop as they please. This is just like a chain-smoker saying that he can quit whenever he wants. He cannot.

The whole point of the term 'addiction' is that it is not under the individual's control. Yes, they need to take steps to get rid of the addiction but it will not be an instantaneous recovery. The sufferer needs to take certain steps, but it is unrealistic to believe that he/she will go on the complete journey of recovery alone.

We have talked about the stigma that comes from people. We have talked about what neighbours or strangers might think about a person with mental illness. However, we have not talked about the stigma that is enforced by the family and friends of a person. This type of stigma, while not very well known, is more potent and harmful than the stigma of society at large.

Take a moment and think about the last time someone approached you with their problems. Think about the last time a good friend came to you and told you about the problems they were facing in their home, at school, in a relationship or in any other domain of life. What did you tell them? Did you listen to their problems and give them support? Did you hear them out and offer possible solutions or give them some other advice?

Now think of another scenario. A friend who has been having problems after a tough break-up comes to you for help. This is the fourth time he is telling you about it. At this point, you are not very interested in hearing about the same problems again. He tells you about how he cries himself to sleep every night, his academic performance has deteriorated and his whole life is a mess. You have heard all this before. Now, you have nothing new to say. You are irritated and in a moment of rage, you shout, "Why are you being such a whiny baby? Just get over it already. It has been so long since you have been crying about the same thing. I am tired of your constant complaining. You need to get a life and find a hobby."

This is where the stigma starts.

Stigma does not always find residence in the thoughts of strangers. Many times, it resides closer to home. It resides in our friends and our family. It is protected by a few rounds of emotional expression. It is more potent and dangerous than a stranger's stigma because it makes the individual lose faith in their first line of defence, that is, their support system. It is harmful because it isolates a person. It is disturbing because it is no different from betrayal. It is what happened to me. It is what happened to Yashasvi. It happens to millions of people around the world.

The problem with it is you cannot put all of the blame on the person who says it. After all, not everyone has what it takes to be a healer. Everyone has a limit to how much they can hear about the same thing. The problem starts when we do not share that someone might be about to cross this limit. Regardless of why the words above are said, the biggest loss happens only to the person who hears them. When person's confidant tells them to 'get over something' even once, they stop seeking their help. He/she starts expecting others to react in the same way.

Being told to 'get a life' could eventually lead to the end of one.

No Knowledge

A little information is dangerous, but you know what is more dangerous?

No information at all.

The biggest competitor for misinformation, as a promoter of stigma of mental illnesses, is having no information. The lack of information is mostly of two types. One is where people do not know that they have the symptoms of a mental illness, meaning a person does not know they might be suffering from a disorder. The other type is where a person does not know who they can approach for help. People do not always recognize that they may be suffering from a mental disorder because these illnesses approach silently and take over gradually. Being sad for a long time takes very little time to develop into depression. Others do not even believe that depression or substance addiction are mental illnesses. For them, mental illnesses only refer to things like schizophrenia where they can label a person 'crazy' or 'unstable.'

Over time, through historic references and misrepresentation by mainstream media, there is a set attitude that mental illness only means having delusions, hallucinations or as some people would call it, seeing and hearing things that are not there. These symptoms are most commonly found in people who have schizophrenia and so the two are connected in the minds of many. Whenever people hear the term 'mentally ill,' they immediately think of schizophrenia-like symptoms.

When the same people hear that people who are mentally ill do not always have hallucinations, they go through a state called cognitive dissonance (Festinger, 1957). Cognitive dissonance is a feeling brought about when the perceptions we hold are challenged by conflicting information. You can think of this as a smoker puffing on a cigarette while he reads about someone dying of cancer. The person knows that smoking causes cancer, but he still likes smoking. There is a conflict every time he smokes. What does he do then? In this situation, there are two options. He either changes his attitude towards smoking, or he ignores the conflicting information and lives in a state of denial.

People who deny the existence of mental illnesses choose to live in a state of denial when they feel dissonance building up in their minds. After all, it is easier to believe that all researchers, doctors and scholars have an agenda instead of questioning your own set beliefs. The only way this can be undone is if we can create stronger dissonance or re-interpret the source of these perceptions. Mainstream media will have to play a major role in doing so. One of these ways would be to make new movies that depict the seriousness of mental illnesses and not promote any stereotypes. Talks on radio or stories with themes of mental health are an option. Print media, visual, audio and all forms of literature are essential in tackling this lack of information.

It is easier said than done though. Movies that accurately depict mental illnesses are tough to execute because we have to build a character who is always at odds with himself. It would have to be a movie where the illness does not define the character, but still shows how much it can affect a person's daily life. This may be a reason why most filmmakers have gone with the easier option and perpetuate the stereotypes giving the audience what they want.

The lack of information does not only mean people do not consider depression or addiction a mental disorder. It also means that sometimes, people do not realize what they are feeling could be the signs of a mental disorder. I was scrolling through 9gag, an entertainment website, when I received a message from a 23-year-old man, Mr. PV. He had been following my work on mental health awareness. He told me his story. He had depression for two years but could not get the help he needed. This was because he did not know he was suffering from depression.

His family had given up on him because he was not being productive or becoming independent.

Mr. PV was sure what he was feeling was just sadness. He decided that he was very lazy, which is why he constantly felt guilty. Thoughts of self-harm and suicide constantly tormented him. He did not do anything again because he thought he deserved it. He only decided to seek help when he saw my interview on NDTV about my struggles with depression. That was when he realized what he was suffering from *could* have been depression and a visit to a counsellor would help. A problem that might have been solved easily had been stretched across years because no one around him knew that a disease like depression exists. This shows how improving mental health awareness can help people come to know there is a place they can go to for help.

This point leads to the second disservice done to people struggling with their minds due to a lack of information or awareness. We saw that Mr. PV was unable to get help because he could not recognize the symptoms and seek help for them at the right time. There are many other people who struggle to find out who they should approach for help. There are many terms used and there is a chance that this causes confusion among people. Psychiatrist, psychologist, clinical psychologist, therapist, counsellor, on and on they go. There are so many terms for people who can help with a mental disorder that people do not understand who they should go to for help.

A psychologist is anyone who has a postgraduate degree in Psychology. A clinical psychologist is a person who has a postgraduate degree in Psychology with a specialization in clinical settings. A psychiatrist is a person who has a postgraduate degree in medicine with a specialization in psychiatry.

A counsellor may or may not be a psychologist. The counsellor will listen to your problems and help you resolve your problems. However, one must not confuse it with guidance. Someone who gives you guidance helps you choose what you value most whereas someone who counsels helps you make changes to avoid the problems you have in life (Gladding & Batra, 2018). A clinical psychologist focuses on more serious problems like psychological disorders, personality issues, etc. They use psychological therapies like psychoanalysis, CBT, etc. The psychiatrist has a job similar to a clinical psychologist. The difference is that instead of psychological therapies, they will use medical interventions like drugs or ECT.

It is only psychiatrists who have the authority to put you on psychological medications. Not every psychiatrist will give you the time to listen to all your emotions and what you are feeling in your day to day life. It is a common complaint that I hear, "The psychiatrist did not even listen to my problems. She just asked what the trouble was and gave me some medicines."

A psychiatrist does not always give you the emotional care that is needed when treating a mental disorder, but they will give you all the biological help that you need. There is also a fear among people when it comes to the use of psychological drugs lest they get addicted or face any untoward side effects. If you are afraid of taking medicines, you can communicate this to the psychiatrist you are seeing. It is important that you realize that you are in control of your treatment and unless the case is an extreme one, you can direct your treatment. Psychiatrists are mostly approached when an illness becomes so severe that a medical intervention is imperative. This makes it harder for the psychiatrist to listen. In most cases, the best option has been to work with a psychiatrist and a clinical psychologist in tandem.

So far, we have talked about how stigma affects mental illnesses and their various sources. To understand how this stigma works, it is important that we understand how it can vary from illness to illness. There are some illnesses that are just considered a mood of life rather than a serious illness. It is also believed that these moods are up to the will of the individual, for example, depressive disorder. These are the illnesses which seem to have a high controllability, but in reality, they are an illness just like the others.

The last kind of stigma, most commonly associated with mental illnesses, is the one where we believe that the sufferer is crazy, dangerous and unstable, for example, schizophrenia. When we look at all the disorders separately, we realize how much the stigma attached varies and this is what makes it so hard to tackle it. An effort to reduce the stigma against mental illnesses will need to acknowledge and have a plan on how it plans to reduce the stigma for all of them instead of using a single approach to reduce the stigma of every mental disorder.

The Schi********Ic

Imagine, how horrifying it will be to have a schizophrenic as head of a state or government.

– A Prominent Psychiatrist from New Delhi, India.

Schizophrenia is one of the most stigmatized illnesses in the world. Generally, people want to keep greater social distance from a person with schizophrenia than from someone with depression (Rossler, 2016). The situation is so bad that even among mental health advocates, it is considered taboo to talk about schizophrenia. Why is it so bad to talk about schizophrenia? Why are even mental health advocates afraid to talk about it? In the past, it was people who had schizophrenia who had to suffer the worst of the atrocities. They were regularly chained, beaten or branded witches and burned alive. In the modern day, someone suffering from schizophrenia is very likely to be distanced by social circles and labelled dangerous or crazy by society.

A very disheartening fact that I came across while reading about schizophrenia was that the fears are not always misplaced. People with severe paranoid schizophrenia are more likely to commit violent crimes than patients of any other illness, which makes their care that much more challenging. The best way to reduce the risk of aggression is with adequate treatment of schizophrenia. (Torrey, 2011)

The next biggest challenge to their care is the stigma attached to it. One would think that if an illness has been known for centuries, nay, millennia, it would have less stigma attached to it. The sad fact remains that those who have this illness are rarely properly cared for. The major proportion of stigma around schizophrenia emerges because it is the prototype of mental illnesses in the general population. Hallucinations, delusions, negative behaviour and suicidal ideation are commonly observed in those who have it. If you step outside your home and ask people to describe a mentally sick person, chances are they will describe someone with schizophrenia. People who insist on not calling depressed people 'crazy' are sometimes, found calling schizophrenics 'loony tunes.'

If we are going to raise awareness on one issue why do we need to put others down? It also stems from ignorance of the fact that different mental disorders carry different stigmas. The quote at the beginning of this section can be found in a book by a prominent psychiatrist from New Delhi. This doctor has written more than a dozen books on the subject. To hear such words coming from a respected psychiatrist disappointed me. It also reinforced my belief that schizophrenia is the most stigmatized illness in the world. He wrote various other gems as well, some of which are presented below.

A mentally ill person cannot attend to his work properly. He becomes a social and economic burden.

A mentally ill person is not only a problem to himself but is also harmful and dangerous for others.

Like so many others, he makes the mistake of not separating the person from the illness. The other arguments he makes are based on science and research. He emphasizes on visiting a psychiatrist instead of a self-proclaimed godman and describes how mental illnesses are not necessarily lifelong problems.

Alas, it is the inaccuracies among facts that lead to problems instead of information that is wholly wrong. When respected authors and psychiatrists are saying things like these, how can we expect a layman to understand our issues?

This leads me to an experience I had with the prevailing literature in the market. I came across a book at the World Book Fair, New Delhi in

January 2019. I was going through all the stalls looking for a book that talks about mental disorders or at least attempts to bust some myths about it. It was one of the two books I found in the whole book fair. I did not visit every stall in every hall, but I put in an intensive effort to dig up a book on the issue. The other book I found about mental health was titled *How to Overcome Depression*. I was immediately attracted to the book and went through it within a day.

The sad thing is that the author confuses depression with extreme sadness and hence, the whole book is based on a faulty premise. My visit to the book fair also reinforced my idea that this book was necessary at the time. I admit that it is possible that with time, many faults will emerge in this book as well, but it is important that those faults are corrected by other literature and not used just to discredit this work. Criticize me, criticize my work but do so with the support of credible research or sound logic. It is not criticism that scares me, but the destructive power of time that does.

* * *

Living with schizophrenia is very, very hard. The first obstacle comes at identifying what is a hallucination and what is not. Ignoring the terrifying hallucinations is a long way away when identifying them is a challenge. It has sometimes been compared to having **nightmares while being awake.** We are terrified of a nightmare even if we know it is one and we know we are sleeping. How terrifying would it be if you saw the same with your eyes open?

In a country like India, where superstitions are rife, it becomes harder for a person with schizophrenia to live. In rural areas, they may have to face forced beatings or exorcisms and in the urban, upper-middle class demographic, they face high levels of isolation from social circles. There have been many instances where an ill person who needed compassion and medical care was tied to a tree or put through cruel rituals in order to *chase the spirits away*. Even in urban areas, people often prefer to go to a faith healer or an exorcist before visiting a doctor for the treatment.

In India, marriage is considered a major event in an individual's life. It is an event that is built up for their whole life. Everyone is expected to get married and if you do not, there must be something wrong with you. Marriages are a big deal in India, whether it is in rural or urban areas. There is always an extravagant expenditure.

People with schizophrenia are often rejected for marriage even by family members. It is advised that the person does not get married and if they do, that they hide their illness from their in-laws. Research carried out by Loganathan and Murthy (2011) to understand what it is like to have schizophrenia in India, and these were some excerpts that researchers reported,

I was to marry my cousin, now after my illness, my relatives have decided not to get her married to me and have given her hand elsewhere. At home also, people don't give me importance, whatever I say has no value at all.

The stigma of schizophrenia, or any other mental illness, is not a philosophical topic. It is something that affects lives and people. There have been cases where a pregnant woman, who had schizophrenia, was forced to abort the baby. If the sick woman went through to full term, a female child was sent back to the woman's family along with her and in the case of a son, the child is taken away from the woman who is then sent back to her home.

People call me all sorts of names and tease me as 'mad' and 'mental'. Even when I am fine they say things about me which unsettles me and I feel bad. My family has abandoned me. Now, I have to live all alone, away from my children.

It is hard enough to face delusions that are created by our own mind. The mind becomes an enemy and there is nothing we can trust. Should we really be piling it up on them with a social boycott and shame? The people who live around someone with schizophrenia are scared.

They are scared because they do not understand what is happening to a person they know well, and people hate what they do not understand.

It is time we clean up the hate and help people understand what is going on in a sick mind. People who are living with it need our support and empathy, not our apprehension and ostracization. Most cases manifest at the age of early adulthood which is usually when we are in college. It is very important that more people are sensitized to identifying the symptoms and seeking help and support.

For how long will the most well-recorded mental illness remain stigmatized?

Not Really III

Illnesses like depression or substance abuse addiction beget a response where people are not willing to accept that they are mental illnesses. You will see people saying that it is a person's choice to be depressed, or that it is due to laziness or inherent inabilities.

This is where Yashasvi's case comes in. His case is a perfect example of how people can have depression even if they have no tangible problems in life or any apparent inabilities. Such a case is largely unheard of because of how rare it is.

Most people today, understand depression is a phase of stress or a mood of sadness. It is seen as something that is temporary and can be gotten rid of with little or no help. There are many radio jockeys who claim to cure depression on a phone call as well. If only that was possible; we would not have the huge burden of depression that India, and the world, faces today. The situation of substance addiction is even worse.

There are many countries where it is not considered an illness legally, and anyone found using drugs is imprisoned instead of being institutionalized. Lawmakers, like the general public, believe that it is under the control of a person to use drugs and if they have strong enough willpower, then it would not be a problem. The sufferers are seen as criminals and it is widely accepted that they need to be kept away from society to keep normal people safe. The problem with this assumption is that it places the addict in an active role in their life. We believe that there is no compulsion on an alcohol addict to drink and therefore, anything that happens must be a choice of their own free will.

Unfortunately, our will is seldom in our own hands. The only time we can say someone is taking a drug or an addictive substance of their own choice is when they take it for the first time. Even then, it is not certain that the decision is always free. High peer pressure and a compulsion to conform to a group are the major contributors to people consuming addictive substances for the first time. I do not intend to make excuses for behaviour that needs to be minimized. What I am trying to do is help people understand the psyche of someone who is addicted so that we can make efforts to ensure that we can fight the menace of substance addiction. There are various theories, which try to explain why there is such a high correlation between substance addiction and mental disorders.

One theory says that people who have a genetic **predisposition** to mental illness are also vulnerable to substance abuse. Also, people who have mental illnesses and alcohol addiction often face stigma from society which marginalizes them. This may lead to co-morbidity, that is the coexistence of two illnesses, where it was not present initially.

This means that people feel that since suffering from a mental disorder is already stigmatized, they can turn to remedies that are stigmatized themselves. After all, how much stigma can an individual face? This leads to an addiction to different substances which is considered a mental disorder according to the DSM as well as the ICD. For the majority of cases, depression and anxiety are found to exist together, but people can have different combinations or mixtures of illnesses as well.

If someone has schizophrenia, it does not mean that they cannot be depressed at the same time. In reality, people who suffer from schizophrenia are more likely to suffer from depression or anxiety. People who are open about their struggles with these disorders talk about all the disorders that they have instead of just one. This makes some people think that these illnesses are being used as mere labels to be different, when the truth is that they are suffering from all of those terrible diseases at the same time.

The second theory says that people who are mentally ill are more **sensitive** to the same amounts of drugs. The third says that ill people consume various substances as a form of **self-medication,** which provides temporary relief from stress. They do not self-medicate to cure a mental illness, but to combat the suffering and the sadness it causes. As we just said, people take alcohol as a form of self-medication.

There is one major problem with this though. A small amount of it may bring short-term stress relief, but it does not treat any of the causes of the stress. In the long term, people who self-medicate need increasingly larger amounts of alcohol or other substances to obtain the required level of dopamine to feel the psychological benefits. This can create a habit, which could lead to increased drinking that could turn into dependence. A person with a mental illness who becomes dependent on alcohol is then caught in a vicious cycle where each problem sustains and even aggravates the other (Alcohol and Mental Illness, Alberta Health Services).

This vicious cycle is deadly and is likely to make people more impulsive and strain their relationships with those close to them. These two effects are devastating for an individual and can increase the chances of suicide. **The one thing people turn to in tough times for salvation, ends up being their damnation.**

Consuming alcohol or other addictive substances is a choice, but it is important that we make this choice after considering its possible consequences.

Stigma, Poverty and Mental Health

India has 70.6 million people living below the international poverty line of a daily wage of USD $1.25. Indian governments have conveniently manipulated the poverty line as per their wish to show fudged numbers of poverty in India.

In recent years, rural electrification is seen as a major driver of poverty rates dropping. Electricity has increased the opportunities for rural people, empowered women and even encouraged girl child education in many places. The electric spark is driving India into the modern age.

Something that has not been investigated or reported on often enough is how severe mental illnesses can lead to poverty. Also, how stigma plays such a destructive role in the lives of people with severe mental illnesses.

The unfair or discriminatory treatment meted out to mentally ill people can result in an obstacle barrier as the patients struggle or are even pushed away from seeking a medical intervention.

The same study that came to the conclusions listed above also highlighted the disproportionate deprivation of resources for women and people from lower castes who suffer from a mental illness. Stigma linked to various marginalized groups has the power to accelerate and intensify exclusion and related discrimination.

Women have to face this stigma in two ways. First, since they are unable to fulfil family roles, they are considered a burden to the family and hence, treated poorly by other family members. Second, the prevalence of superstitions in Indian society makes people believe that women who are mentally ill are under the evil influence of demons or spirits and must be treated through faith rather than through counselling and medicines.

The reserved classes (SC/ST/OBC) have to face further stigma when it comes to accessing education centres or job opportunities. Even though reservations and various governmental policies have been put into place to reduce the stigma, they have largely been ineffective or disproportionate. This perpetuates a cycle of powerlessness and dominance over the people from lower castes. This is then further intensified for people with mental illness.

It is clear that a negative feedback loop exists. Stigma reinforces mental illnesses which then lead to more stigmatisation. This is particularly more evident in people from lower castes and women (Bakhshi, Mishra and colleagues, 2014).

Another aspect is the shame and stigma felt by the primary care givers of the sufferers. This includes things like feeling embarrassed or ashamed of being associated with people who are mentally ill. Mentally ill people are sometimes even shunned by their own families and this leads to homelessness and poverty for them. Even if they belong to highly educated and resourceful families, the threat of social exclusion and being pushed to the side lines of the family remain major threats for sufferers.

This brings me to a question that I ask myself often. Must a lack of financial resources also mean that we are empathically bankrupt as well?

The Western Contradiction

In well-developed nations, the crisis is of a similar magnitude, but it faces challenges that are often the opposite of those faced in developing countries. The USA and UK face a massive mental health crisis with regular reports of suicide or PTSD in veterans, but they face the challenge of focussing solely on the biological aspect of these disorders, and not enough on the psychological and social ones. As we have already discussed, treating a biopsychosocial illness only through biology will not be a sustainable solution. The US in particular faces the widespread medicalization of mental disorders.

Many recognizable faces like Prince Harry and Prince William have been talking about mental disorders and trying to break the taboo on the same. Across the Atlantic, we see Lady Gaga, Miley Cyrus and many other celebrities talking about the need to open up about mental illnesses like depression and break the stigma that surrounds them.

The death of Robin Williams, Chester Bennington, Kate Spade and Anthony Bourdain by suicide shocked everyone across the world because these personalities usually seemed happy and joyous. The idea that many have taken from these tragedies is that mental disorders can happen to anyone irrespective of their economic well-being but sadly, some people have derived the idea that mental disorders only happen to the rich. They see depression and suicide as a luxury that someone who is struggling to feed his family cannot afford but that is an idea that is verifiably false. It has been proved through research that those who belong to poor families are significantly more likely to suffer from mental disorders and have more thoughts of suicide than those who are comparatively well off.

The problem is that a suicide in a poor household does not get nearly as much attention as the death of a celebrity. It is only when the poor die by the thousands that someone takes notice of their lives. A good example would be the farmer suicides that occur in almost every part of India on a daily basis. The suicide of farmers only becomes an issue when it happens regularly and it brings about temporary solutions like a loan waiver at best. In reality, a poor man dying by suicide would not qualify as news for anyone. A poor man's life is cheaper after all.

While we use the media to tackle the stigma of mental health, we need to pay a lot of attention to the contextualizing of the terms we use as well. If you ask an auto-driver if he feels depressed or if he feels bipolar, you would be faced with a blank look since chances are that they do not even know what the words mean. On the other hand, if we ask them if they feel empty on the inside or if they do not enjoy the things they used to earlier, we are more likely to get a meaningful answer that can help us understand the true extent of this emergency.

How do we fight this two-pronged attack of stigma on mental health care?

The Pincer Move

The strategy to fight against such an attack has to be dual as well. When it comes to educating people about mental disorders, putting the general public in touch with people who have fought these illnesses in the past, or continue to do so, is a must. This will make the people realize that the sufferers are human beings who have been struck with a horrible disease. It will help people separate the illness from the person and lead to a more humane view of the victims.

It has also been found that people change their attitude more when the information we give them is in contrast with their pre-existing views. This means that if we can find people who have suffered from schizophrenia or major depressive disorder, but have managed to get a hold of their symptoms they can act as a bridge between the two sections of society. These 'human bridges' will bring the knowledge and experience of mental illnesses to the mainstream and lead to a society where mentally ill people are better understood, empathically approached and socially accepted.

A word of caution is that the people who try to be the bridges between the two sections will have to face a lot of questions and doubts from both sides. There will be questions about their motives, their agendas, their history and everything in between. It is possible that there will be a time when they will be looked at with scrutiny and mistrust but only through ardent honesty can these doubts be overcome. Throughout history, those who have tried to bridge a gap between two different groups of people has been scrutinized. These differences may be small or large. There is always a resistance to assimilating and accepting new people. Even if there is no apparent harm in learning something new, people tend to have a resistance to a group of people who they see as the 'other' people. It is the job of every mental health activist to ensure that there is as little of this resistance as possible.

The goal of the mental hygiene movement as we see it today, is to assimilate with society, ensure people seek medical help and not to carve out our own separate space in the mainstream and then think about seeking help. We must not separate ourselves from the mainstream or see each other as part of a monolithic group with one thought cycle. It is imperative that we become a part of the mainstream and continue to maintain our ideological diversity. Once we manage to assimilate with the general public, we can work on changing things.

The Path Walked Before, NACO

Presently, one in four people will have a mental disorder at some point in their life. We have already talked about the global burden of mental disorders, and how it is costing governments across the world trillions of dollars in lost productivity. The foremost challenges to improvement in these respects is the stigma and the lack of information that people and institutions possess. In order to improve this situation, governments across the world will have to take a leaf out of the campaigns for AIDS and dengue awareness carried out in developing nations.

The National AIDS Control Organization (NACO) was set up by the Ministry of Health and Welfare, India in 1992. The programme has since worked massively to increase awareness about AIDS, its prevention and de-stigmatizing the disease as a whole. The program has an annual budget of Rs. 2064.65 crore which is estimated to be around USD $300 million. The fourth phase of this program, NACP-IV has a set budget of Rs, 13,415 crore, which amounts to almost USD $2 billion! It has been an extremely successful programme which has led to more people getting tested for AIDS and those who suffer from it being treated by their peers. You can regularly hear ads on the radio or in print media which talk about how important it is to get screened for AIDS and that this screening is available with full confidentiality and free of any costs. The day when we might hear the same being said about mental disorders like depression or schizophrenia is still far away. It is something that needs to grow in order to bring a meaningful change.

The Ministry of India and the governments of all developing countries need to start national level programmes that will address mental illnesses directly. Once a programme has been started, it is important that governments are also willing to back it up with proper funding. NACO has a budget of a little less than USD $300,000,000 and that is due to the contribution and donation of various global agencies as well as the central government. You would be surprised to know that a mental health programme at the national level already exists in India.

It has been in existence for nearly a decade longer than the NACO programme, but it has not had as much impact as the AIDS control movement. Why do you think that is? The reasons behind this lack of impact from the National Mental Health Programme (NMHP) are complex and touch the roots of administrative insincerity, corruption, a lack of will to act and a lack of resources and knowledge at its very core. The NMHP works under the Director General of Health Services (DGHS). The DGHS also controls various other programmes which work on leprosy, tuberculosis and other public health issues. The DGHS then works under the Ministry of Health and Welfare. The NACO, on the other hand, works directly under the Central Ministry and is hence, well-funded and regulated. Over a period of around four decades, the NMHP has created district-level infrastructure in almost all the districts of every state although it is not a blanket cover yet.

Sadly, the NMHP is dying a slow death. In the latest Union budget presented in 2019, its funding was cut from Rs 50 crore To Rs. 40 crore. (~$5.8 Million). The government has stopped believing in this programme and it would be better if we could invigorate the mental health movement with a new national level programme.

The fact that despite a limited budget, the NMHP has been able to build a basic infrastructure at such a large scale is commendable, but there is one thing that is lacking. People do not know that this kind of help exists and is supported by the government. This means that right now we need a push to create awareness among the public on how they can avail services for treatment of mental illnesses in their very own districts. In order to do this, we will need the help of a medium that

has long been at odds with the mental hygiene movement, the media.

The Superpowers of Media

In the past, the media, both print and visual, has largely contributed to the stigmatization and misinformation being spread about mental illnesses. A person holding their head in excruciating pain has become the prototype of a mentally ill person. It is as if the people who have a mental illness are perennially suffering from a headache. People in the media would be surprised to know that you rarely see someone behaving like that.

Television shows and movies have depicted the mentally ill as violent and deranged. You can understand this with a simple experiment. If you use any online streaming service to search for the words, 'mentally ill,' 'mental health' or 'mental illness.' Most of the suggestions that come up are likely to be about a violent crime and their perpetrators. These could be docu-series or a documentary. Some of the search results will be about an individual struggling with suicidal thoughts and acting out or someone who has already died by suicide (13 Reasons Why is an appropriate example). It is almost as if the people in media houses believe that someone who is mentally ill must either be a criminal or suicidal (or has a really bad headache).

There is another category of the mentally ill that exists in the media world. It is taking a character who has certain personality quirks and branding them with a suitable mental illness. A recent example of this was Hotstar, a streaming service in India similar to Netflix. They had recently bagged the streaming rights to a highly popular sitcom which follows the story of six friends. A character on this show, let us call her, MG, is very particular about keeping everything clean and organized. She likes her house being arranged a certain way and she likes cleaning things up. The people over at Hotstar proudly aired a short promo where they talked about how this show had started a 'trend' for catchphrases, bromance and OCD. It was as if before MG became a popular character, OCD did not exist and since then it has become 'cool' and 'fun' to have it.

The promo was aired on TV channels regularly and its YouTube upload had 450,000 views within six days. Within six days, this promo impressed hundreds of thousands of people and gave them the idea that OCD is a trend that was started by this popular sitcom. When I submitted a complaint, Hotstar quickly took the ad down but the damage had already been done. To give you some perspective, it took my blog nearly two years to reach 50,000 views and this promo reached almost 10 times as many people in one week!

The reach that print and visual media enjoys is humongous compared to the reach of a blog or even the most prominent mental health organizations in India. It is with this in mind that we need to realize that if we plan on having a meaningful long-term change in the perception and understanding of mental health in the general public, we need to take the media's assistance. We need ads running on radios, televisions and newspapers (of all languages) simultaneously to generate a discussion and demand for knowledge on this subject. Health care providers and the media, particularly television, generally tops citizens' list as a source of health information (Altman and colleagues, 2001). The people at NACO were smart enough to understand the potential of the media and use it to the benefit of the general public. It is time that the people working for mental health start doing the same as well.

The next question that arises now is how do we get the media on our side? The answer is simple. Media, like any other business works either for money or for the government. We can either have a large-scale investment from private organizations and individuals or we can get the government to start something similar to NACO for mental health. The NMHP has been mostly focussed on infrastructure building and now that has been achieved, we need to move to the next phase of getting people into these services. NACO was pro-active in seeking the help of local NGOs who had already been working to prevent the spread of AIDS. There are various organizations doing the same for mental health as well but we need a central agency or organization to bring them all together.

NACO has already been working on drug-addiction since contaminated syringes are a common pathway for the spread of AIDS. It is important that we adapt the next programme for mental illnesses and then launch it. NACO took the step to distribute condoms at little or no charge to rural people in order to promote safe sex. When it comes to mental health, we need to spread awareness about stress management to rural people in a way that they assimilate it quickly.

A small example of how the media can be used for good comes from the #NotAshamed campaign that was carried out by The Live Love Laugh Foundation around Mental Health Day, 2018. It was a campaign that ran for less than a week and had very little airtime. The promos were hardly 10 seconds long but with a recognizable face like Deepika Padukone, the famous Bollywood actress, the impressions and impact it made was equal to, if not more than, what I have been able to achieve in two years of the same work. The campaign, though short-lived, was an encouraging one since I noticed how open people were to the idea of mental health. The time is ripe right now for India and other developing nations to invest more in it and work towards building a more efficient and mentally healthy population.

The Long-Term Solution

Changes to educational curriculums are fundamental to having a mentally healthy society. The role of media and a central organization for mental health would be to spread awareness among the general public but we also need to make changes at the grassroots level in order to have a long-term impact.

There is an ongoing debate in the UK about giving children regular mental health classes and putting them through regular mental health check-ups in order to improve the dire situation we are currently in. There have been some doubters about teaching children about mental health, but their arguments mostly stems from either disinformation or a lack of understanding.

Classes on mental health do not mean that children will be taught about what depression is or what schizophrenia is. They are too young to understand the intricacies of these disorders and giving them lessons on this could increase the rates of self-diagnosis and self-stigma. After all, even those with a graduate degree in Psychology are introduced to these disorders in their final two semesters. It is important to have a basic understanding of Psychology concepts in order to understand their disorders. The classes on mental health will have a socio-emotional approach where the focus will be on teaching young people how to recognize their emotions, express and manage them. It will also include exercises that build resilience and improve the capacity to face stress in life.

The next challenge to this idea is choosing the stage at which we give them these lessons. Teenagers are one of the most vulnerable groups to mental disorders, but if we wait for them to become vulnerable before we teach them, chances are that it will too late by then. We need to have these classes in the pre-teen years when a child is about to or has recently, hit puberty. Grades four to seven emerge as the most appropriate ones for this exercise. Once the time of a course has been decided we need to think about how we will assess a person's performance in these subjects.

If we put too much pressure of these classes, it is possible that we end up creating another subject that only haunts a student instead of helping them develop. If we put too little pressure, chances are that most students would pay little attention since it wouldn't carry any academic weight. The best option is to have it as a supplementary paper similar to Computer Science for these classes. A paper in Computer Science has practical classes, a practical assessment and a short theory paper. More weightage is given to practical understanding over memorizing theory.

Dr. Samir Parikh, Director of The Fortis National Mental Health Programme and Department of Mental Health and Behavioural Sciences at Fortis presented similar ideas in an article he wrote for a national daily,

Being mindful of such a curricular inclusion does not necessarily entail an additional number of academic classes or teaching hours. Instead it could involve more experiential and fun-learning techniques which are enjoyable for both teachers as well as students. This serves the dual purpose of equipping young minds with the necessary skills to improve their overall quality of life in the future, as well as building their resilience to deal with the world and its challenges in the years ahead.

He concluded by saying that,

…the objective of introducing a mental health curriculum is to encourage help-seeking behaviour, especially in connection with mental health. It is through the training of young children and adolescents during their prime years that we can improve their own psychological well-being.

If we manage to scale-up the awareness projects and reach each and every parent, we will be at an ideal stage where emotional intelligence and resilience is seen as a skill that is necessary to succeed in the future world. It will not carry a lot of academic weight with it, but excelling at it will be appreciated by parents and teachers alike.

For a 10-year-old, being appreciated by their parents and teachers is all the encouragement it takes to imbibe a skill.

The Disorganized Ant Colony

First they ignore you, then they laugh at you, then they fight you and then you win.

These were the words of Mahatma Gandhi when he was talking about how one can bring about a social change. It came at a time when India was mounting a struggle for independence against a repressive British rule. Since then, various efforts have been made to map the various stages of a successful social movement. They include educating the public about an issue, mobilizing public support, proposing bureaucratic changes and then enforcing them.

For the mental health movement, we are at a situation where we have an average infrastructure and various laws in place for mental health care. We are mostly lacking in enforcing these laws and making people aware of these services.

In India as of now (late 2018), we have various small organizations working to increase awareness about mental health in their own way. Some people use pictures and visual aids whereas others, like me, use content generation mediums such as blogs and videos to tell people about mental health.

We still lack a central or umbrella organization that can help us coordinate our efforts and get them to a wider audience. Right now, we are like a bunch of small ants working in different directions to reach the same goal. We also have many organizations and individuals who have a sincere desire to increase awareness, but they lack a book they can refer to in order to understand what mental health means and how we can work to improve the situation on the ground.

Due to the lack of popular literature, these individuals end up pursuing Psychology which then reinforces the wider belief that only those with a Psychology background talk about mental health. It is a perennial cycle and one that this book tries to break. The aim of this book is to bring the idea of mental health to the general reader. One who does not have a background in Psychology.

Pinel revolutionized how people look at the mentally ill in the 1790s. He made people believe that those troubled by their own minds did not need to chained or beaten. He convinced people that care and compassion can work. I am trying to bring about another paradigm change in the present. Psychiatric patients are not dangerous people. They are not people who are violent. They are people...who are people...like us.

The Future: Utopia or Apocalypse?

Where does the future of mental health care lie? Will it continue to be a stigmatized subject or will there be a time when a person will not have to be ashamed to ask for emotional support? If, against all odds, we end up achieving the goal of a mentally healthy society, what will it be like?

It is widely believed that a low quantity of mental health professionals like psychiatrists or psychologists is a major barrier to improving the state of mental health care in India, but it is not necessarily the case. The WHO (2007) has proposed a pyramid for the levels of mental health care. This includes the possible centres of treatment of patients as well as the role of the community. They have also proposed that in the future, we need to move away from psychiatric institutes and work towards community care under the guidance of trained professionals to care for the mentally ill.

Self-care is found at the base of this pyramid of care. It demands the lowest resources and is used most commonly. It is important to stress that the WHO is not asking you to keep your problems to yourself. Instead, it professes the importance of accepting the need for care and seeking it from family and friends first.

Informal community care, the next step of the pyramid, is seeking help from informal community resources like faith healers, religious heads, NGOs and so forth. These informal community care services do not need to come from professional health care exclusively. Instead, there needs to be a dynamic relationship between the two. Religious or NGO heads must have the pragmatism to refer someone they have not been able to help, to a medical professional. These services cannot form the 'core' of mental health care, rather it plays the role of a facilitator to the formal care systems. They are a part of the pyramid, not a cornerstone of it.

The next part of the pyramid is the promotion of community-based services and provision of psychiatric care in general hospitals. According to this, it is important to have a psychiatry wing in general hospitals rather than having specialized psychiatric care centres. The integration of mental health care is easier said than done.

Often, the stigma attached to mental health makes the staff unwilling to work in hospitals with a psychiatric wing. The staff also needs to be trained thoroughly to ensure that the patients receive the best quality of care possible. This will help with early identification and treatment of illnesses, which would ultimately make higher levels of care obsolete. If people at risk are identified in time, the chances of them becoming seriously ill reduce drastically.

Specialized psychiatric facilities are those that are dedicated to treating mental illnesses. I, along with many other advocates for mental health have asked for more centres of excellence to be built in order to provide the best quality of care possible. In the future, these institutions will likely be obsolete as we move from a centralized, medical treatment to a social, community-based healthcare that puts emphasis on the psychological and social aspects of the illness.

It was found that institutionalizing patients did not help with their recovery as was previously thought. It leads to further isolation of people from society which is not healthy in the long term. The WHO says that we need to limit the number of mental hospitals and, promote self-care and community mental health services; both, formal and informal. **The future of mental health care lies in the community.**

When we try to envision what the future of humanity will be, we have various visions available. Some see us finding our place among the stars and move from being based on one planet to being a multiplanetary species. Others predict a dystopian world where people will be living in shelters and under constant threat of nuclear radiation. A technological future promises a society which is maintained by robots and leaves humans to achieve their true potential. The discipline of mental health does not promise a future of this kind.

We do not promise that a mentally-healthy population will never be sad or feel like crying. Neither do we say that mental illnesses will be wiped from existence. We propose neither apocalypse nor utopia in the future. What we propose is that we will live in a world where people are more in touch with themselves and the people around them. A world where resilience is celebrated, emotional turmoil is not looked down upon, and where seeking help is encouraged. A future where a person is not identified with their illness; where visiting a psychiatrist does not cause a commotion in their community. We work towards a world where we will be allowed to express our emotions regardless of our sex and a world where hope will be found in every corner.

A future that will be content with itself.

Section VI

The Dull Golden Bird

An Indian Context

India is, in the most simplistic terms, a country of contradictions. It is home to the richest man in Asia as well as a large share of the world's poorest people. It is a nuclear state and an emerging economy with prevalent caste and sex discrimination. It has been rightly said that whatever you can say rightly about India, the opposite of it is equally valid (Robinson, quoted by Sen, 2005). The country is also marred by a large divide between rural and urban areas. No entity can better explain this gulf than the cow.

In the rural areas, a cow is seen as an asset. The milk is used for feeding young calves and sold to neighbouring households. The manure is used as a fertilizer in the fields and the urine is used as a domestic disinfectant. Once the cow is past her milking days, she can be sold to a slaughterhouse for a good price, although, this particular practice has been banned by the central government in the last few years. In urban areas, the cow is seen as a nuisance to traffic. They can be seen roaming about, feeding on garbage. How does a rural asset end up becoming a hindrance in an urban area?

It is in these contradictions that the country has continued to progress despite being up against the odds at most times. Whether it was the communist insurgency of 1948 or the various separatist movements that propped up in 1970s and 80s, India has found her way.

Dr. Bhimrao Ambedkar, the Father of the Indian Constitution gave a very apt warning in 1949 about the future of the country. He said India is now a land where equality exists in law but not in practice. When it comes to the topic of mental health, it becomes a daunting task to come up with an idea that will cover all the land of 7th largest country in the world.

India is full of different cultures, sub-cultures, languages and their dialects but if there is one thing that is the same for every Indian is a sense of belonging towards the country and its people. Apart from sharing a feeling of unity, we also have a sense of identifying ourselves with a group. The sense of belonging could be primarily to those who belong to the same caste, same profession or the same language.

Regardless of what the uniting factor is, we always like to belong. This is something that is considered as part of a collectivist culture that is endowed in us over centuries. In countries like the USA or the UK, the culture is more focused on the individual instead of the group. The identity of the self in these countries is given more importance and achieving personal goals is considered more important than reaching the goals of the community. This culture is called an individualistic culture.

No culture is necessarily better than the other. A person who has grown up in a collectivistic country like India will naturally consider it superior to an individualistic culture, but it is important that we understand that all cultures come with some positives and negatives. These cultural differences lead to subtle differences in how the world is perceived and how viewpoints or belief systems are formed. In India, a sincere, honest and friendly personality is considered 'good,' whereas in the USA, someone who is assertive and strong, traits important for competitive success, are considered superior.

The differences in culture also lead to differences in how a society is formed and how an individual's psychological processes work. Just as psychological processes exert fundamental influences on culture, so too does culture exert fundamental influences on basic psychological processes. (Lehman & Schaller, 2004)

This means that there are different perceptions and understandings of the same event. This should help you understand why there is such a gulf in the western (USA, Canada, West Europe) and eastern (India, China, Japan) societies. It also explains the need for varying strategies to tackle the stigma of mental illnesses in different cultures.

India was known as the Golden Bird in olden times. In the present, the Golden Bird has dulled. She does not exude brightness and confidence like it did. The Golden Bird has lost her shine.

As things stand, the state of mental health in India is not very encouraging. The suicide rate in India is 16.3 against the global average of 10.5 per 100,000 population (WHO, 2016). The rate has come down marginally in the last few years but the progress is not as quick as it needs to be. On an average, a student dies by suicide every hour in India. Farmer suicides are often the topic of debate on news channels, but the solutions proposed for them are myopic at best. The worrying issue is that despite claiming so many lives, people are not willing to talk about mental disorders and their care.

Most people do not do so, because they do not care. Others do not do it because they simply do not know how threatening the situation is. Politicians are always the first ones to whip up a nationalistic fervour, and use the army and soldiers as a tool for political leverage. The sacrifice of a jawan is used in public rallies to draw public support, but the true motive of the politicians using these sacrifices is for an ascent to power.

I do not believe for one second that our politicians believe or try to work towards ensuring as few army casualties as possible. In the period between 2007–12, more soldiers died from suicide than from cross border fire (Sharma, 2015). In the last seven years, more CRPF paramilitary forces died by suicide than those that died from terrorist attacks (Ministry of Home Affairs, India). Despite this, you would never hear a politician talk about the need for sensitization to mental disorders and management of suicidal tendencies. That topic is convenient to ignore because people do not want to talk about it anyway.

Cognitive comfort is given a higher priority than the life of a human being.

We can have as many programmes and organizations as we want in India. The truth is that the central government is the most resourceful organization in the country. Most of the organizations that work for mental health awareness today, are either non-governmental or not-for-profit. This approach is considered ideal because it puts service to society above profits but in the long run, every NGO and Not-for-Profit setup ends up becoming a slave to its donors. As soon as the money dries up, the work is stopped.

The Schizophrenia Research Foundation, India had set up a community mental health programme in Thirupuror, Chennai in 1989. The programme was funded by a research centre in Canada. Due to a lack of funds, the programme was shut down in 1999. In 2005, a follow-up study was done to understand the present condition of people seeking treatment earlier.

The programme had around 440 patients; 185 of them had psychotic disorders. Out of these 185 patients, only 15% (!!) continued their treatment after the programme was closed. Out of the patients who had dropped out of treatment, 75% showed signs of acute psychosis. They were in urgent need of treatment, but they had no means of doing so. Thirty-two patients had wandered away from their homes and were untraceable. No suicides were 'officially' reported. (Thara, 2008)

A lack of funds affected people who needed help. They were given a ray of hope, but then it was snatched away. A community had come together to help people, but it could not stay together due to a lack of expert guidance. Money may not buy happiness but for these people, money could have given them an inkling of sanity and optimism.

Mental Health Programmes need money. We can either create businesses that generate money and then use this money for our cause, or, we could get the government of India to back us. As we had seen in the case of HIV/AIDS, an effort by the central government ended up halving the spread of AIDS throughout the country.

As of 2017, India spends Rs. 520 crores on mental health. In a year, the government spends around Rs. 1,100 on your health. Out of this, only Rs. 4 goes to your mental health. Think about it for a second, Rs. 4 in a year. That's all. That's all the money we have. That's all the money mental health gets. USD $0.06 is all the money that the government of India spends on your mental health in a year. (Mental Health Atlas, WHO, 2017)

When going through India's profile and comparing it with other developing countries, the only positive I could find was that at least the data existed in India. Other nations had taken the convenient route of claiming a lack of data in their profiles. We are willing to accept our shortcomings and now, it is time that we start on fixing them.

Mental disorders claim significantly more lives and are more prevalent than chikungunya and malaria. Mental health gets only Rs. 520 crores per year whereas for tuberculosis, India has put aside Rs. 4400 crores. We have already discussed what the figure for HIV/AIDS is. It is due to a lack of initiative and will on the part of the administration because like the people they serve, they do not really know or care about mental illnesses.

Cultural differences influence our social world and our Psychology. We had earlier talked about how mental illnesses have a biopsychosocial model instead of a simple biomedical one. Culture has a huge influence on two of the three components of a mental illness. It is important that we take the cultural differences into account while trying to treat a mental illness. Something that is not well appreciated in the world of psychiatry, so far is how cultural context plays an important role on the psyche of each individual.

India is a land of many cultures all of which are remarkably different from the culture of the USA or Europe. It is important that we also adapt the tools and techniques that we use according to the cultural context we are going to use them in. It is with this in mind that I discuss the concept of community mental health interventions in an Indian context.

Community Mental Health

Indian society has been a collectivistic one for centuries. The main focus in our society is not on each individual, but a group of individuals collectively. We often see people talking about the importance of collective action rather than individual efforts. Hence, it is pretty important that we look into the possible role that the community around the sufferer can play in their treatment.

India is a country of about 1.2 billion people as of 2011. The current estimate puts the population at somewhere around 1.35 billion. No matter how much the government tries, it is hard to believe that a time will come soon enough, when every rural village will have access to high-quality healthcare.

Mental health care, hence, fares even worse than normal health care. It is important that to ensure mental wellbeing of all individuals, we have grassroots programmes that would lead to a trained counsellor in every village. One such effort was made in Maharashtra and later in Gujarat by the name *Atmiyataa.*

Atmiyata Project

Atmiyata means shared compassion in the Marathi language. The project was first implemented in various villages of Maharashtra as a pilot project for a period of 24 months. There is a nearly 85% treatment gap in India for mental disorders. This means that nearly 85% of the people who have been identified as suffering from a mental disorder do not seek or receive the medical assistance they need.

To reduce this said gap, an NGO in Canada funded the *Atmiyata* project. They started reaching out to self-help groups (SHGs) and Farmer's Clubs (FCs) in rural areas to sensitize them to common mental disorders. These small community groups often play a very important role in other social movements too.

Under the supervision of Dr. Kaustabh Joag, various *Atmiyata* champions and *mitras* (friends) were chosen in the villages under the purview of the study. These champions were trained in identifying the symptoms of common and severe mental disorders. The training also included providing basic treatment and support and working as a mediator between the people who needed further help and mental health professionals.

The *mitras* were trained to some lesser extent. This included identifying stress in individuals and disseminating information on wellbeing and available treatment options. They also made people more aware about available government schemes to support poor families financially. *Atmiyata*, hence, also tackled poverty in rural areas.

The main thing that separates *Atmiyata* from other community interventions is the use of informative videos in tackling mental health ignorance. The organizers used various interviews to identify the most recognizable social workers and actors in rural areas.

These social workers and actors that made many videos, which talked about the different aspects of mental health. They also talked about how seeking support or treatment for them is not a shameful thing. These videos also had breaks in between so that the champions and *mitras* could discuss the topics portrayed and explain them to people. You can watch the videos on YouTube for free.

Another feature that set *Atmiyata* apart and made it so effective is that it used local community members to help people in emotional distress. It did not impose the concept of mental illnesses on the villagers.

It, instead, invited members from within the community to participate and make society healthier and more empowered.

The uncomfortable truth is that these community intervention programmes are hard to scale up and suffer from a lack of funding after a while. Moreover, the need of cooperation from local psychiatrists and community members may not always be a given. It may suffer stiff resistance in some areas.

The pilot study in Maharashtra from 2013–2015 was a huge success none the less. The *Atmiyata* project is now going to be implemented in Mehsana, Gujarat as well. This will take quality mental health services right to the grassroots level.

Another very important thing in the rural Indian setting is the prominence of religious figures and the influence they have over locals. Many priests are often approached for life problems in search of a solution. Many community intervention programmes which have been carried out, have emphasized the importance of these religious figures. They are asked to listen to each person's problem that approaches them and encourage them to visit doctors or psychologists for additional help. We criticize the superstitions that some priests spread around but we must not ignore their power in rural settings. A word of caution though is always necessary. Rural areas are ripe with self-proclaimed Godmen and *tantriks* who claim to cure mental illnesses through spells and magic. Awareness needs to be spread about the falsehoods of these fraudsters too. Religious figures are important allies in rural areas, but we must choose our allies carefully.

India is a land of many cultures. We are different from the traditional roots, from which clinical psychology emerges in the western world. If we want to make a more meaningful and deeper impact, we must try something different. Community interventions are the way ahead in my opinion, when it comes to treating mental disorders in rural India.

It is unrealistic to believe that the people in rural India will undergo a paradigm shift quickly when it comes to mental illness. It is also important to note that a society is more likely to change when the change is brought about by someone from within the society. The responsible people of a community need to act as the connecting links between better health care and its access to the common man. We can change the situation, but none of us can do it alone.

I cannot change the world. We can.

Psychiatrist Stigma

Statistics say that there is one psychiatrist for 300,000 people in India. So what is it that is causing this huge gap between requirement and availability? I believe it is quite easy to blame the education system, the medical education or migration of doctors out of India, but there is another aspect that has not been considered at all. It is the **stigma associated with being a psychiatrist in India.**

There is a lot of explicit stigma associated with visiting a psychiatrist. A survey conducted by psychiatrists on 924 people showed that most of them did not even consider psychiatrists for consultation or treatment of mental illness (Zeiger, 2017). People just do not want to visit psychiatrists.

A big problem lies in the fact that even undergraduate medical students are not exposed to psychiatry properly. There is a compulsory posting of 15 days in a psychiatric ward, but many colleges fulfil that just on paper and it no surprise that there is a low ratio of students willing to be psychiatrists. Moreover, a two-week posting has been found to be insufficient to change someone's opinion about the subject.

Psychiatry is not an independent examination subject and the attendance for its classes is not compulsory. In a study carried out in a medical college in North India, it was discovered that only 5% of students had attended more than 50% of their theory classes throughout the semester (Gulati, Das & Chavan, 2014). The same study also explored the attitude towards psychiatry as a career option. It was found that psychiatry was being discouraged by family members, peers and its negative outlook among the general public turned many students away from the profession. Students believed that psychiatrists are respected less in society unlike their non-psychiatric peers. It was also found that they had prejudices against those choosing psychiatry and considered them odd, eccentric people. (Lingeswaran, 2010)

They only chose psychiatry as a career when they could not pursue other specialities. Even then, they felt uncomfortable being around mentally-ill patients. The sad thing is that the same students said that the mentally ill deserve our compassion, care and can be treated. More than 73% students also believed that if our hospitals had well-trained doctors and nurses that they could be cured. Diffusion of responsibility is truly a beautiful thing. Most students believed that there need to be more psychiatrists, but very few of them chose to be one.

Another study was conducted in two medical colleges in South India and only 13% students saw psychiatry as a career option. Many interns have reported to have felt fear when attending to a patient who is mentally ill (Kodakandla, Nasirabadi & Pasha, 2016). If someone who is being trained to attend to the mentally ill feels fear (despite no history of violence), hate (although very rarely), then there is something fundamentally wrong in how we teach our future doctors and how the mentally ill are viewed.

There are also lots of misconceptions about psychiatrists. These are further reinforced by inaccurate depictions of psychiatrists in film and media. An analysis of 26 movies was done between 2001–2010, that included 33 psychiatrist characters – 42.4% percent of them were incompetent and 39.4% breached professional ethics. Only 30.3% were shown to have an accurate diagnosis (Banwari, 2011). Psychiatrists are misconstrued in movies often. This inevitably leads to a negative perception among the general public.

The depiction of ECT, lobotomy, forced medication as a mode of punishment or management of psychosis has been highlighted in various Bollywood movies like Raja, Damini, Khamoshi, Jewel Thief, Rat aur Din, etc.

In India, psychiatrists have been framed as villain in old Bollywood movies. (Bhattacharayya, 2016)

The social stigma attached to being a psychiatrist is immense. It is somehow considered that psychiatrists are 'crazy.' The belief that only the 'crazy' treat other 'crazy' people is simply not true. We do not expect neurologists to have a brain problem and neither do we think our dentists have teeth filled with cavities. Yet, there is a perception that psychiatrists have a problem. This does not include the belief that psychiatric medicines are money-making techniques used by 'Big Pharma' to get money. This is a big problem, which is not discussed very often. Even among advocates of mental health awareness, there is very little appraisal of this situation. We always encourage people to remove the stigma around mental illness, but **are we willing to de-stigmatise the profession of psychiatry as well?**

Deadly Unemployment

In January 2019, the Business Insider published a report which said that the unemployment rate in India is at a 27-month high. Nearly 11 million jobs had been lost in 2018 and most of these were in the rural areas. According to the NSSO, unemployment is at 45-year high. The problem with stats on the same is the existence of parallel economies in India. One of these is formal and the other is informal. It is very hard to predict the employment status in the informal sector, which affects the validity of all the data quoted.

It is no surprise that the increasing rate of unemployment has an effect on the mental health of the job seekers. For most of the people around, everything that we need is mostly provided by employment. This includes financial security, decent social status and many other factors. These needs range from physical ones to psychological needs. It is only when we lose employment that we realize how big a role it plays in our life.

After the global recession of 2008, there were large-scale layoffs in companies across the globe. The USA was the worst hit country, and this led to a huge economic crisis on a global level. Another unforeseen consequence of this was elevated working hours for the physicians in the UK. People were finding it hard to cope with the shame and stress associated with unemployment, even the prisons found themselves at almost full capacity. Crime rates increased as people decided to resort to illegal means to meet their needs. This was mostly observed in developing nations. Some people even committed petty crimes to go to jail. They said prisons provided stable accommodation and food. These were two things that were hard to find in times of unemployment.

Between 2005 to 2015, the number of suicides citing unemployment as a reason grew by 2000% in Madhya Pradesh, India. The number was at 29 in 2005, but 579 in 2015 according to the National Criminal Record Bureau. (It is interesting in itself that the records for suicide are stored at the crime bureau. Until 2018, suicide was legally a crime in India.) In order to curb this alarming increase, the government made a very shrewd move that brought down the rate of suicide dramatically.

They stopped releasing the data on suicides due to unemployment!

The number of deaths by suicide due to unemployment in 2016 and 2017 has not been released. It seems that the administration knows something is wrong and they would rather keep everyone wilfully ignorant than take steps to help. Sadly, this problem is not isolated to Madhya Pradesh. There are reports from almost every state in India, where youngsters have made suicide pacts with other friends or expressed their suicidal tendencies to close ones.

By this time, you must also be thinking of the role a society can play in this situation. We have already discussed how our social environment can affect our biology and psychology. It is due to the shame attached to unemployment that people start having suicidal thoughts. While unemployment is not something that should be made desirable, why must we make it shameful to the point that people feel like a burden to their family?

Why is employment so important for our psychological well-being and what effects does it have on us? Two scientists, S.V. Kasl and V. Cobb, tried to answer this question through their research. They have done a lot of work on the impact of losing a job on the health of a person. They mainly focused on physical health but had also taken into account the mental aspects of well-being. Their most interesting discovery was that people who are re-employed have lower levels of stress and strain than people had never lost their jobs in the first place. A job helps us satisfy our creative urges, promotes self-esteem and provides opportunities for achievement and self-realization. This makes the tendency that when a person is 'dismissed' or 'fired,' that they struggle with low self-esteem and inhibited social skills understandable. It is expected to increase anxiety and depression.

It could also lead to physical consequences if the pursuit of a job fails over a long period of time. A place of employment helps us settle in a routine and keeps our mind distracted. I will not say that a depressed person would be cured if they had a job, but I am saying that a person who has a job is less likely to suffer from major depressive disorder or an anxiety disorder. There is a correlation, but no causation has been established yet.

Social support also has been found to have an effect on the unemployed. People who were supported by close ones and friends, during times of unemployment had lower levels of depression and anxiety. People often try to solve a lack of social support by visiting physicians or psychologists. Doctors hence, are not always curing physical or mental illnesses. Sometimes, they end up being channels to vent the stress of a person.

In socialist countries, basic universal income is an economic norm. It was found that a universal income does reduce the financial stresses of an individual but it cannot fulfil the psychological needs of the human mind. In developing nations, lack of employment remains a huge burden on the work force. There are contributions of the crumbling education system and government apathy here as well, but the ultimate loser is the individual. Education, poverty, healthcare systems and even prison administrations are influenced by the rate of unemployment. Jobs and a lack of them affects many issues directly or indirectly. It is time we started tackling the issue straight on instead of playing petty politics over it.

Being a Man

Being a man comes with a lot of terms and conditions in today's world. A man is expected to fulfil every expectation of the family. He is supposed to be strong and focused. It is not like a man to display any emotions or cry. They have the pressures of the world on them but no means to express the effect these pressures have on them. Emotional expression is not very common in male groups. Any negative emotion is either laughed off or ignored. It leads to a situation where a man is in severe turmoil, but practically has no social support mechanism. We have been discussing the importance of social surroundings, which is another challenge for any man suffering from a mental illness. While men are significantly less likely than women to be diagnosed with depression, they are the victims of the majority of suicides. (Picinelli & Wilkinson, 2000)

The lack of socio-emotional support could also lead to engaging in antisocial behaviour. The Vogue Magazine released an ad a few years back with a prominent Bollywood star. The ad showed young boys being told that "Boys don't cry", "Boys are brave", "You are a tiger and tigers don't cry". The ad then went on to show a man beating his wife with a blank face. She concluded by saying, "We tell our boys not to cry. Why don't we tell them that boys don't make others cry?"

How about we let our boys cry instead?

What would have a more long-term impact on young boys? Telling them through force, beatings and scolding that they should not make others cry or letting them cry when they feel like it? If emotional expression is encouraged at a young age, it could lead to higher empathy in adulthood. A boy who is allowed to cry as a child will be less likely to make others cry in adulthood.

Masculinity does not need to be just about suppressing all emotions and appearing strong. The strength lies in accepting who we are and how we feel. Men have stayed strong for too long. They have suppressed their feelings too long. How about we let our boys cry?

How about we let our boys feel?

Some Rays of Hope

As we had discussed before, there are many small organizations in India that are trying to do their bit in making India a mentally healthier society. The lack of an umbrella organization to direct these organizations is apparent, but even without them they have managed to make an impact in their own way.

A good example is the Mental Health Foundation (MHF, India) founded by Prof. Nand Kumar in 2003, before he joined as faculty in the Department of Psychiatry, AIIMS, Delhi. Prof. Nand Kumar has been trained in Psychiatry from AIIMS, Delhi and working in Neuropsychiatry and Behavioural sciences for decades. Currently, he is the Professor in-charge and Chief of Centre for Advanced Research and Excellence in Neuromodulation and Mental Health, AIIMS, Delhi.

He believes mental health needs to be perceived by people in positive way and always extended support from AIIMS, Delhi to MHF (India) for all meaningful activities of MHF (India). The MHF (India) has introduced the concept of Mental Health Festival on occasion of World Mental Health Day (10th October) since the last five years that is being celebrated in the AIIMS, Delhi in association with department of Psychiatry, AIIMS, Delhi.

The organization had filed a Public Interest Litigation (PIL) in 2011, with the Delhi High Court seeking the decriminalization of suicide.

Seven years later, in 2017, the Mental Health Care Act, decriminalized suicide and helped establish MHFI as one of the leading names in mental health awareness in India. Prof. Nand Kumar is a man who started Psychological First Aid for prisoners in Tihar Jail, that is first time in India and the second in the world.

Currently, MHF (India) has its representative in Central Mental Health Authority of Govt of India.

In Mumbai, an initiative by the name, 'Apni Shala,' founded in 2013 has been working to build social and emotional skills in children from the lower socioeconomic stratum. The most encouraging thing I saw among the people at Apni Shala was that they had a preventive approach to mental health.

Children from poor backgrounds find it hard to receive education and even if they do, the quality is generally low in most parts of the country. In the words of the CEO, Amrita Nair,

"The idea began by thinking of how stories can be used to create a safe space for children to have conversation about their own life stories, the joys, struggles that come with it. Hence, we started by having sessions in a BMC (Brihanmumbai Municipal Corporation) school where we would read stories and then have life skills building sessions that followed. Gradually our focus narrowed in terms of implementation and in language. The essence still remains to create a safe space for children to talk about things that really matter to them in their lives. The structure and design of the programme is aimed at promotion of mental health and wellbeing. However, in the long term the programme will grow to become a full school mental health program that provides access to both preventive support as well as interventions as the context requires."

A similar approach is being used by many other organizations throughout India. The organizations have a lot of experiences and knowledge to share and since they work in separate areas of the country, try to imagine how invaluable the knowledge would be if they could get a chance to share it with each other. They would know how to approach people from different communities, different strategies and different methods of achieving the same goal. It is from the synthesis of these two ideologies that a better, more efficient method will emerge that can be possibly scaled up to the whole country.

Sambandh Health Foundation, a Not-For-Profit in Gurugram takes a curative approach to the mentally ill and tobacco addicts. They believe that all the stakeholders of a mental illness need to be strengthened to have a community-based approach to help a person recover and contribute to the society. They recently tied-up with the Government of Haryana and are scaling up their operations to the whole state. Sambandh Health has an ambitious team where the role of every individual is well defined.

I had the honour of visiting their office recently. It is an awe-inspiring sight to see so many people working meticulously, in tandem to ensure the well-being of those who are mostly ignored. They have been working day and night for a long time and it will not be long before they become a nationally prominent name in the healthcare of tobacco addiction and mental illness.

An individual we have gotten to know very well over the course of this book returns in this section. Yashasvi, the 19-year-old boy who was struggling with severe clinical depression is now creating mental health awareness. He is using his blog and a YouTube channel to generate more content for people to access and learn about mental health. There are thousands of other individuals and organizations that are doing the same thing and slowly, things are changing. Slowly, we are becoming more humane and less mechanic. Slowly, we are becoming more empathic and less apathetic.

The Curious Case of Yashasvi

As we move towards the end of this book, we shall return to the boy with whom we started. Yashasvi presents a rare anomaly in the large number of people suffering from mental illnesses. There was no apparent reason for him to be depressed. His academic achievements were being used as a model for other students to follow, when he started showing the first signs of depression. He was socially active and had his fair share of friends.

In the two years that he was depressed, he was consumed by a vacuum of emptiness. The people around him had emerged as barriers instead of facilitators to recovery. There was no conscious effort from him to get better either. He accepted it as his personality and believed that this was how he would die, miserable and alone.

Extreme sadness manages to break many people and leaves them unable to return to their previous levels of happiness and activity. Clinical depression, mild or moderate, makes people unable to have many, if any, feelings for the rest of their lives. What chances did Yashasvi have to emerge from his very severe clinical depression? Therapy had not worked for him and neither had medicines. Even electro-convulsive therapy did not have any long-lasting effects. The odds of this young boy reviving himself were dwindling with each passing day and yet, today we see him working actively to make his society a more sensitive and empathic one. How did this turn around happen?

There are two unconventional answers to this question, a movie and social media.

Yashasvi had been a superhero fan for most of his life and there were many mainstream movies being made on them between 2015 and 2017. He was a fan, but he had never been obsessed with these fictional characters. In 2016, at the peak of his depressive state, he watched a movie he had been waiting for, for years. The movie inspired him and gave him the slightest of hope. It is interesting to note that the movie in discussion was widely criticized by critics and audience alike. Yet, it managed to have an ever-lasting impact on the youngster. The movie released in the early part of the year and for all he knew, he was not going to make it to the end of it. He had suicidal thoughts every second of every day and he did not believe that he could keep fighting off those thoughts for a whole year. This movie changed that. It made him want to make it to the next year, to see the sequel. The movie did not stop his suicidal thoughts or his urges to harm himself, but it made him feel a little less lonely. When he walked on the roof of his hotel, he would listen to the movie's soundtrack. The emptiness was still there. The loneliness was still there, but he had one tiny ray of light. One small thing that he looked forward to in life.

The movie gave him hope that people can return even from the darkest corners. It made him believe that men are still good. It was a movie he could relate to. He saw superheroes he could connect with. He saw all-powerful beings facing the same conflicts that he did. It made him want to live for just a little longer.

To you, this may seem like an outlandish reason to stay alive. Why would anyone want to live for just another movie? Why would anyone be so attached to characters that are not even real? Fiction sometimes, makes us feel more than reality ever could. After all, we do not choose where we get our inspiration from.

For Yashasvi, this movie gave him a new lease on life. Although, he did not realize it at the time. In the 18 months between this movie and its sequel, his life would change for the better. Social media would play a central role to that.

By February 2017, Yashasvi had been through 12 prescribed rounds of ECT. The effects were starting to wear off and he was again, plunging into that vacuum of hopelessness. He had tried everything, but nothing had worked. He was desperate for help. He needed something, anything, to hold on to for the lightest shade of hope. In his desperation, he took a step that finally paid off. He shared his story on his Facebook account.

Love and support poured in from all directions. His teachers from second grade and those from his coaching classes came together to share what they felt about him. They shared stories of how he is used as a role model by many teachers, and how he serves to inspire many of his juniors. The people he knew from school, even those he barely knew, shared their thoughts and tried to display how much of an effect he had had on other people without knowing it.

Until then, he was convinced that his life did not matter. He was certain that his death would not have any effect on any living soul, but things changed when he read the comments. His phone was ringing with calls, buzzing with messages and lighting up with notifications. All of them filled with support and affection, with care and compassion.

In that moment, he felt like he was alive.

In that moment, he felt like he mattered.

In that moment, he felt.

That one moment of emotional arousal and social support was all he needed to turn things around. He started working on himself. He became more active on social media and talked to more people on texts. Twelve days later, he launched his blog at www.knightofsteel.com, as an homage to the superheroes who had made him stay alive until then. Since then, everything has had an upward trend for him. He decided to give up on medicine as a career and took up psychology. He believed the course would be lighter and give him more insight into what psychology is all about. In 2018, he wrote his first book titled *The*

A-Z of Mental Health and started his own YouTube channel. He also wrote the book you are reading right now.

Today, Yashasvi finds himself surrounded by a faithful group of friends, a loving family and a supportive social setting. He cracks jokes (although very bad ones). He smiles. He laughs. He loves. For all the things that have happened to him.

He is not done with life just yet.

THE END

References

18.6 million without jobs in India this year, unemployment rate to stand at 3.5 per cent in 2019. (2018, November 09). Retrieved from https://www.indiatoday.in/education-today/jobs-and-careers/story/unemployment-growing-concern-indian-students-1384978-2018-11-09

ANDERSON M. (2003) Journal of Psychiatric and Mental Health Nursing 10, 297–306 'One flew over the psychiatric unit': mental illness and the media.

Annexure I, Manpower Development Schemes, Directorate General of Health And Services, 2014–15.

Anthony Painter, Jake Thorold and Jamie Cooke, "Pathways to Universal Basic Income," RSA Action and Research Center, February 2018.

Armstrong, E. (2015). A Study on the Relationship Between Emotional Intelligence and Mental Illness Stigma. Minnesota: Walden University.

Armstrong, T. (2018). MI Theory and Its Critics. In Multiple intelligences in the classroom(4th ed.). Alexandria, VA, USA: ASCD.

Aruna, G., Mittal, S., Yadiyal, M.B., Acharya, C., Acharya, S., & Uppulari, C. (2016). Perception, knowledge, and attitude toward mental disorders and psychiatry among medical undergraduates in Karnataka: A cross-sectional study. Indian journal of psychiatry, 58(1), 70–76. doi:10.4103/0019-5545.174381

Attitudes to mental health problems and mental wellbeing, British Social Attitudes (2015).

Avasthi, A. (2016). Are social theories still relevant in current psychiatric practice? Indian Journal of Social Psychiatry, 32(1), 3-9. doi:10.4103/0971-9962.176685

Babalola, E., Noel, P., & White, R. (2017). The biopsychosocial approach and global mental health: Synergies and opportunities. Indian Journal of Social Psychiatry, 33(4), 291-296. doi:10.4103/ijsp.ijsp_13_17

Baker, C.A. (2014, September 22). Father Jofré. Retrieved from https://carolineangusbaker.com/tag/father-jofre/

BANYARD, P. AND GRAYSON, A. (2000) Introducing Psychological Research; Seventy Studies that Shape Psychology, 2nd Edition. London: Macmillan.

Baron, R.A. & Misra, G.(2014). Psychology New Delhi: Pearson Education.

Barrett L.F. (2009). The Future of Psychology: Connecting Mind to Brain. Perspectives on psychological science: a journal of the Association for Psychological Science, 4(4), 326–339. doi:10.1111/j.1745-6924.2009.01134.x

Bearak, B. (2001, August 07). 25 Inmates Die, Tied to Poles, In Fire in India In Mental Home. Retrieved from https://www.nytimes.com/2001/08/07/world/25-inmates-die-tied-to-poles-in-fire-in-india-in-mental-home.html

Benning T.B. (2016). No such thing as mental illness? Critical reflections on the major ideas and legacy of Thomas Szasz. *BJPsych bulletin, 40*(6), 292–295. doi:10.1192/pb.bp.115.053249

Berk, Bernard. (2015). Labeling Theory, History of. International Encyclopedia of the Social & Behavioral Sciences. 10.1016/B978-0-08-097086-8.03161-5.

Bertolote J. (2008). The roots of the concept of mental health. World psychiatry: official journal of the World Psychiatric Association (WPA), 7(2), 113–116.

Bhattacharyya, Ranjan. (2016). Indian Media and Mental Illnesses: Beyond the Love Hate Relationship. J. Adv. Res. Psychol. Psychother. 2016; 3 (1). 2. 1-7. 10.5958/2395-180X.2016.00024.4.

BI India Bureau. (2019, January 07). India witnessed its highest unemployment rate in 27 months at 7.38% in December, says CMIE. Retrieved from https://www.businessinsider.in/india-witnessed-its-highest-unemployment-rate-in-27-months-at-7-38-in-december-says-cmie/articleshow/67418218.cms

Bolton D. (2013). Should mental disorders be regarded as brain disorders? 21st century mental health sciences and implications for research and training. World psychiatry: official journal of the World Psychiatric Association (WPA), 12(1), 24–25. doi:10.1002/wps.20004

Bowers, E.S. (2012, March 14). Are You Guilty of Stigmatizing the Mentally Ill? Retrieved from https://www.everydayhealth.com/depression/are-you-guilty-of-stigmatizing-the-mentally-ill.aspx

Boyd, K.M. (2000). Disease, illness, sickness, health, healing and wholeness: Exploring some elusive concepts. Medical Humanities, 26(1), 9-17. doi:10.1136/mh.26.1.9

Br, Sahithya & Reddy, Rajakumari. (2018). Burden of mental illness: a review in an Indian context. International Journal of Culture and Mental Health. 1-11. 10.1080/17542863.2018.1442869.

Br, Sahithya & Reddy, Rajakumari. (2018). Burden of mental illness: a review in an Indian context. International Journal of Culture and Mental Health. 1-11. 10.1080/17542863.2018.1442869.

Branscombe, N.R., & Baron, R.A. (2017). *Social psychology*(14th ed.). Harlow: Pearson Education Limited.

Broman, N. (2018, August 31). U.K.: New Government Plans for Mental Health Support and Education in Schools. Retrieved from https://www.tieonline.com/article/2422/u-k-new-government-plans-for-mental-health-support-and-education-in-schools

Brown, R. (2018, April 25). Biographical notes: Henri Tajfel biography project. Retrieved from http://www.sussex.ac.uk/psychology/henri-tajfel/biographical

Building Bedlam – Bethlem Royal Hospital's early incarnations. (2016, February 13). Retrieved from https://historic-hospitals.com/2016/02/13/building-bedlam-bethlem-royal-hospitals-early-incarnations/

Busby, E. (2018, July 19). Mental health education to be made compulsory in England schools. Retrieved from https://www.independent.co.uk/news/education/education-news/mental-health-education-england-compulsory-schools-sex-relationships-children-a8453596.html

Bynum, W.F., Porter, R., & Shepherd, M. (1985). The Anatomy of Madness: Essays in the History of Psychiatry: Volume 2 - Institutions and Society(Vol. 2). Routledge.

Caddell, J. (2018, July 15). Understanding the Stigma Around Mental Illness. Retrieved from https://www.verywellmind.com/mental-illness-and-stigma-2337677

Carey, B. (2012, September 11). Dr. Thomas Szasz, Psychiatrist Who Led Movement Against His Field, Dies at 92. Retrieved from https://www.nytimes.com/2012/09/12/health/dr-thomas-szasz-psychiatrist-who-led-movement-against-his-field-dies-at-92.html

CDC: 10 most important public health problems and concerns. The CDC's National Center for Injury Prevention and Control updated its Prevention Status Reports Monday, which ranks the biggest public health issues in all 50 states and the District of Columbia. (2016). Retrieved from https://www.beckershospitalreview.com/population-health/cdc-10-most-important-public-health-problems-and-concerns.html

Chawla, J.M., Balhara, Y.P., Sagar, R., & Shivaprakash (2012). Undergraduate medical students' attitude toward psychiatry: a cross-sectional study. Indian journal of psychiatry, 54(1), 37–40. doi:10.4103/0019-5545.94643

Cherry, K. (2018, October 27). Psychologist Robert Sternberg and Triarchic Theory of Intelligence. Retrieved from https://www.verywellmind.com/robert-sternberg-biography-1949-2795530

Chi, T. (2017, August 22). Is Addiction a Mental Illness? - #1 Mental Health Blog. Retrieved from https://www.talkspace.com/blog/addiction-mental-illness/

Christiansen, J. (2009). Social Movement and Collective Behavior: Four Stages of Social Movement. EBSCO Research Starter, 1-7.

Christine Stevenson 'Robert Hooke's Bethlem' in *Journal of the Society of Architectural Historians*, vol.55, no.3 (1996), p. 257

Christine Stevenson 'Robert Hooke's Bethlem' in *Journal of the Society of Architectural Historians*, vol.55 no.3 (1996), pp. 254-275

Ciarrochi, J., Deane, F.P., & Anderson, S. (2002). Emotional intelligence moderates the relationship between stress and mental health. Personality and Individual Differences, 32(2), 197-209. doi:10.1016/s0191-8869(01)00012-5

Ciccarelli, S.K., Meyer, G.E. & Misra, G. (2013). Psychology: South Asian Edition. New Delhi: Pearson Education.

Claeson, M., & Haacker, M. (2009). HIV and AIDS in South Asia: An economic development risk. Washington, DC: World Bank.

Corrigan, P.W., & Watson, A.C. (2002). The Paradox of Self-Stigma and Mental Illness. Clinical Psychology: Science and Practice, 9(1), 35-53. doi:10.1093/clipsy/9.1.35

Corrigan, P.W., & Watson, A.C. (2002). Understanding the impact of stigma on people with mental illness. World psychiatry: official journal of the World Psychiatric Association (WPA), 1(1), 16–20.

D. Mayer, John & Salovey, Peter. (1993). The Intelligence of Emotional Intelligence. In Intelligence. (4th ed.) Ch. 17. 433-442. 10.1016/0160-2896(93)90010-3.

Davydov, D.M., Stewart, R., Ritchie, K., & Chaudieu, I. (2010). Resilience and mental health. Clinical Psychology Review, 30(5), 479-495. doi:10.1016/j.cpr.2010.03.003

Deacon, Brett. (2013). The biomedical model of mental disorder: A critical analysis of its validity, utility, and effects on psychotherapy research. Clinical psychology review. 33. 10.1016/j. cpr.2012.09.007.

Deep, D. (2018, March 10). 'Manifold rise in suicide due to unemployment in Madhya Pradesh' - Times of India. Retrieved from https://timesofindia.indiatimes.com/city/bhopal/manifold-rise-in-suicide-due-to-unemployment-in-madhya-pradesh/articleshow/63248273.cms

'Dengue cases in India up by 11,832 over last year.' (2017, July 31). Retrieved from http://www.theweekendleader.com/Headlines/10527/-dengue-cases-in-india-up-by-11-832-over-last-year-.html

Derryberry M. (2004). Today's health problems and health education. 1954. American journal of public health, 94(3), 368–371.

DiMaggio, P.J. (1997). CULTURE AND COGNITION.

Downey, L.A., Johnston, P.J., Hansen, K., Schembri, R., Stough, C., Tuckwell, V., & Schweitzer, I. (2008). The relationship between emotional intelligence and depression in a clinical sample. *The European Journal of Psychiatry,* 22(2), 93-98. http://dx.doi.org/10.4321/S0213-61632008000200005

Dozois, David. (2012). Influences on Freud's Mourning and Melancholia and its contextual validity. Journal of Theoretical and Philosophical Psychology. 20. 167-195. 10.1037/h0091208.

Earley, P.C., & Ang, S. (2003). Cultural intelligence: Individual interactions across cultures. Stanford, CA: Stanford University Press.

Earley, P.C. (1993). East Meets West Meets Mideast: Further Explorations of Collectivistic and Individualistic Work Groups. Academy of Management Journal. 36. 319-348. 10.5465/AMBPP.1991.4976900.

"Economic Cost of HIV and AIDS in India," (with Sanghamitra Das and Abhiroop Mukhopadhyay), in Markus Haacker and Mariam Claeson (eds.), HIV and AIDS in South Asia: An Economic Development Risk, chapter 4, 123-154, The World Bank, Washington, DC, 2009

Erwadi, an incurable malady. (n.d.). Retrieved from https://www.thehindu.com/thehindu/2001/08/26/stories/13260611.htm

Extracts from the Report of the Committee Employed to Visit Houses and Hospitals for the Confinement of Insane Persons, With Remarks, by Philanthropus', The Medical and Physical Journal, 32, August 1814, pp. 122–8, quoted in Scull 1993, p. 113

FACT SHEET – WORLD AIDS DAY 2018, UNAIDS

Farreras, I.G. (2019). History of mental illness. In R. Biswas-Diener & E. Diener (Eds), Noba textbook series: Psychology. Champaign, IL: DEF publishers. DOI:nobaproject.com

Fenton, K. (2016, August 4). Mental health - our attitudes and awareness. Retrieved from https://publichealthmatters.blog.gov.uk/2016/08/04/mental-health-our-attitudes-and-awareness/

Fenton, K. (2016, August 4). Mental health - our attitudes and awareness. Retrieved from https://publichealthmatters.blog.gov.uk/2016/08/04/mental-health-our-attitudes-and-awareness/

Figueroa, M.D., & Alvarez, M. (2015, October 21). Mental Illness in the Dark Ages. Retrieved from https://www.hercampus.com/school/albizu/mental-illness-dark-ages

From Bethlehem to Bedlam – England's First Mental Institution. (n.d.). Retrieved from https://historicengland.org.uk/research/inclusive-heritage/disability-history/1050-1485/from-Bethlehem-to-bedlam/

Funds and Expenditures, NACO

Gaertner, Lowell & A. Insko, Chester. (2000). Intergroup discrimination in the minimal group paradigm: Categorization, reciprocation, or fear? Journal of personality and social psychology. 79. 77-94. 10.1037/0022-3514.79.1.77.

Galvani, S. and Livingston, W. (2012) Mental Health and Substance Use – Essential Information for Social Workers. A BASW Pocket Guide. Birmingham: BASW.

Ganeshkumar P, Murhekar MV, Poornima V, Saravanakumar V, Sukumaran K, Anandaselvasankar A, et al. (2018) Dengue infection in India: A systematic review and meta-analysis. PLoS Negl Trop Dis 12(7): e0006618. https://doi.org/10.1371/journal.pntd.0006618

Ghai, S., Sharma, N., Sharma, S., & Kaur, H. (2013). Shame & stigma of mental illness. Delhi Psychiatry Journal, 16(2), 293–301.

Gill, C. C. (2017, September 12). We shouldn't teach children about mental health. Retrieved from https://health.spectator.co.uk/we-shouldnt-teach-children-about-mental-health/

Gladding, S.T., & Batra, P. (2007). *Counseling: A comprehensive profession.* Pearson Education India.

Gleadell, J. (2018, November 07). The Case Against Mental Health Awareness Raising. Retrieved from https://areomagazine.com/2018/11/07/the-case-against-mental-health-awareness-raising/

Global AIDS Monitoring 2018, UNAIDS

Gohain, M.P. (2017, March 22). CBSE unveils new exam format for classes VI to IX - Times of India. Retrieved from https://timesofindia.indiatimes.com/home/education/news/cbse-unveils-new-exam-format-for-classes-vi-to-ix/articleshow/57761979.cms

Gold, M., & Richards, H. (2012). To label or not to label: The special education question for African Americans. In *Paper presented at educational foundations conference.*

Goldhill, O. (2016, October 02). Bedlam: The story behind the London mental hospital that came to mean hell on earth. Retrieved from https://qz.com/798351/bedlam-the-story-behind-the-london-mental-hospital-that-came-to-mean-hell-on-earth/

Greif, Avner. (1994). Cultural Beliefs and the Organization of Society: A Historical and Theoretical Reflection on Collectivist and Individualist Societies. Journal of Political Economy. 102. 912-50. 10.1086/261959.

Gritti, Paolo. (2017). The bio-psycho-social model forty years later: a critical review. Journal of Psychosocial Systems. 1. 36-41. 10.23823/jps.vlil.14.

Growing unemployment, a big reason to worry! (2019, January 08). Retrieved from https://www.thehansindia.com/posts/index/ Editors-Desk/2019-01-08/Growing-unemployment-a-big-reason-to-worry/471075

Guha, R. (2017). *India after Gandhi: The History of the World's Largest Democracy*. London: Macmillan, an imprint of Pan Books.

Gulati, P., Das, S., & Chavan, B.S. (2014). Impact of psychiatry training on attitude of medical students toward mental illness and psychiatry. Indian journal of psychiatry, 56(3), 271–277. doi:10.4103/0019-5545.140640

Gupta, G & Kumar, S. (2010). Mental health in relation to emotional intelligence and self-efficacy among college students. Journal of the Indian Academy of Applied Psychology. 36. 61-67.

H Banwari, Girish. (2011). Portrayal of psychiatrists in Hindi movies released in the first decade of the 21st century. Asian journal of psychiatry. 4. 210-3. 10.1016/j.ajp.2011.07.001.

Ha, T. (2016, January 03). How should we talk about mental health? Retrieved from https://ideas.ted.com/how-should-we-talk-about-mental-health/

Haakenstad, A., Moses, M., & Dieleman, J.L. (2018). Comparing estimates of spending on health and HIV/AIDS. The Lancet, 392(10158), 1622. doi:10.1016/s0140-6736(18)32164-0

Health Data- India (http://www.healthdata.org/india)

Henri Tajfel - Social Psychologist - biography. (n.d.). Retrieved from https://www.age-of-the-sage.org/psychology/social/henri_tajfel.html

Hermesauto. (2018, September 21). Mentally-ill Maryland shooter shot herself twice in head after deadly warehouse rampage. Retrieved from https://www.straitstimes.com/world/united-states/mentally-ill-maryland-shooter-shot-herself-twice-in-head-after-deadly-gun

Hindustan Times. (2017, August 13). For the army to be an effective fighting machine, mental health of soldiers must be a priority. Retrieved from https://www.hindustantimes.com/editorials/for-the-army-to-be-an-effective-fighting-machine-mental-health-of-soldiers-must-be-a-priority/story-5tr63kGBAOYKnLqHmo625N.html

HIV and AIDS in India, Avert (https://www.avert.org/professionals/hiv-around-world/asia-pacific/india)

Horwitz, Allan & C Wakefield, Jerome & Lorenzo-Luaces, Lorenzo. (2016). History of Depression. 10.1093/oxfordhb/9780199973965.013.2.

Howard Gardner (www.howardgardner.com)

Howard Gardner, multiple intelligences and education. (2013, April 25). Retrieved from http://infed.org/mobi/howard-gardner-multiple-intelligences-and-education/

Howard Gardner. (n.d.). Retrieved from http://pz.harvard.edu/who-we-are/people/howard-gardner

The History of Bethlem, p.248 quote from Bethlem Court of Governors Minutes

India Is the Nation of The Most Unemployed in The World: Labour Bureau Statistics. (2018, April 04). Retrieved from https://www.outlookindia.com/website/story/india-is-the-nation-of-the-most-unemployed-in-the-world-labour-bureau-statistics/310545

India, UNAIDS (http://www.unaids.org/en/regionscountries/countries/india)

J. Sternberg, Robert. (2005). The Theory of Successful Intelligence. Revista Interamericana de Psicología. 39. 10.1177/026142940001500103.

Joaquin Sorolla y Bastida - Artworks. (n.d.). Retrieved from http://www.the-athenaeum.org/art/list.php?m=a&s=tu&aid=373

John, E.A. (2017, November 11). 1 in 3 Indians thinks shrinks are mentally ill, says survey - Times of India. Retrieved from https://timesofindia.indiatimes.com/india/1-in-3-indians-thinks-shrinks-are-mentally-ill-says-survey/articleshow/61601592.cms

Joseph, N. (2010, July 01). Mental Illness as a Social Construct. Retrieved from https://artsci.washington.edu/news/2010-07/mental-illness-social-construct

Karp, David & Jin, Nobuhito & Yamagishi, Toshio & Shinotsuka, Hiromi. (1993). Raising the Minimum in the Minimal Group Paradigm. THE JAPANESE JOURNAL OF EXPERIMENTAL SOCIAL PSYCHOLOGY. 32. 10.2130/jjesp.32.231.

Kim Robinson, (2006) "Mental Health: Facing the Challenges, Building Solutions," International Journal of Migration, Health and Social Care, Vol. 2 Issue: 2, pp.46-47, https://doi.org/10.1108/17479894200600019

Kodakandla, Krishna & Nasirabadi, Minhaj & Shahid Pasha, Mohammed. (2016). Attitude of Interns towards Mental illness and Psychiatry: A study from two medical colleges in South India. Asian Journal of Psychiatry. 22. 10.1016/j.ajp.2016.06.008.

Kumari, S., Mishra, S.N., Chaudhury, S., Singh, A.R., Verma, A.N., & Kumari, S. (2009). An experience of community mental health program in rural areas of Jharkhand. Industrial psychiatry journal, 18(1), 47–50. doi:10.4103/0972-6748.57860

Lacasse, J.R., & Leo, J. (2015). Challenging the narrative of chemical imbalance: A look at the evidence (pp. 275-282). In B. Probst (Ed.)., Critical Thinking in Clinical Diagnosis and Assessment. New York: Springer

Lazarus, S. (2018, October 17). Therapist vs. Psychologist vs. Counselor » Dr. Steven A. Lazarus. Retrieved from https://www.drstevenlazarus.com/2011/11/14/therapist-vs-psychologist-vs-counselor/

Leo, J., & Lacasse, J. R. (2007). The Media and the Chemical Imbalance Theory of Depression. Society, 45(1), 35-45. doi:10.1007/s12115-007-9047-3

Lingeswaran A. (2010). Psychiatric curriculum and its impact on the attitude of Indian undergraduate medical students and interns. Indian journal of psychological medicine, 32(2), 119–127. doi:10.4103/0253-7176.78509

Link, B.G., & Phelan, J.C. (2013). Labeling and stigma. In Handbook of the sociology of mental health (pp. 525-541). Springer, Dordrecht.

Link, B.G., Phelan, J.C., Bresnahan, M., Stueve, A., & Pescosolido, B.A. (1999). Public conceptions of mental illness: labels, causes, dangerousness, and social distance. American journal of public health, 89(9), 1328-1333.

Link, B.G., Yang, L.H., Phelan, J.C., & Collins, P.Y. (2004). Measuring mental illness stigma. Schizophrenia bulletin, 30(3), 511-541.

Link, B., & Phelan, J. (2001). Conceptualizing Stigma. Annual Review of Sociology, 27, 363-385. Retrieved from http://www.jstor.org/stable/2678626

Linn, M.W., Sandifer, R., & Stein, S. (1985). Effects of unemployment on mental and physical health. American Journal of Public Health, 75(5), 502-506.

Livianos, Lorenzo & Sierra, Pilar & Moreno, Luis. (2010). The Foundation of the First Western Mental Asylum. The American journal of psychiatry. 167. 260. 10.1176/appi.ajp.2009.09030371.

Loganathan, S., & Murthy, R.S. (2011). Living with schizophrenia in India: gender perspectives. Transcultural psychiatry, 48(5), 569–584. doi:10.1177/1363461511418872

Lopez-Ibor, Juan J. (2008). The founding of the first psychiatric hospital in the World in Valencia. Actas españolas de psiquiatría. 36. 1-9.

Manderscheid, R.W., Ryff, C.D., Freeman, E.J., McKnight-Eily, L.R., Dhingra, S., & Strine, T. W. (2009). Evolving definitions of mental illness and wellness. Preventing chronic disease, 7(1), A19.

Manwell, L.A., Barbic, S.P., Roberts, K., Durisko, Z., Lee, C., Ware, E.L., & McKenzie, K. (2015). What is mental health? Evidence towards a new definition from a mixed methods multidisciplinary international survey. *BMJ open.*

Markov, S. (2017, June 10). Philippe Pinel – The Father of Modern Psychiatry. Retrieved from https://geniusrevive.com/en/philippe-pinel-the-father-of-modern-psychiatry/

Marshall, P.J. (2009). Relating Psychology and Neuroscience: Taking Up the Challenges. Perspectives on Psychological Science, 4(2), 113-125. doi:10.1111/j.1745-6924.2009.01111.x

Masculinity and mental health STRATEGIES FOR IMPROVING HEALTH AND SOCIAL CARE, Swedish Association of Local Authorities and Regions, 2018

Matthews, Steve & Dwyer, Robyn & Snoek, Anke. (2017). Stigma and Self-Stigma in Addiction. Journal of bioethical inquiry. 14. 10.1007/s11673-017-9784-y.

Mattoo, Surendra & Sarkar, Siddharth. (2012). Validation of Hindi version of perceived stigma of substance abuse scale. Indian Journal of Social Psychiatry. 28. 117-120.

McCann, Joseph J. (2016) Is mental illness socially constructed? Journal of Applied Psychology and Social Science, 2 (1). pp. 111.

Mechanic, D. and McAlpine, D.D. (2002). The Influence of Social Factors on Mental Health. In Principles and Practice of Geriatric Psychiatry (eds J. R. Copeland, M. T. Abou-Saleh and D.G. Blazer). doi:10.1002/0470846410.ch17

Mental Health ATLAS 2017 Member State Profile- INDIA, World Health Organization, 2017

Mental health: a state of well-being, WHO, 2014

Ministry of Health and Family Welfare, India (www.mohfw.gov.in)

Mishra, A., Mathai, T., & Ram, D. (2018). History of psychiatry: An Indian perspective. Industrial psychiatry journal, 27(1), 21–26. doi:10.4103/ipj.ipj_69_16

Murthy R.S. (2017). National Mental Health Survey of India 2015-2016. Indian journal of psychiatry, 59(1), 21–26. doi:10.4103/psychiatry.IndianJPsychiatry_102_17

Murthy S.R. (2001). Lessons from the erwadi tragedy for mental health care in India. Indian journal of psychiatry, 43(4), 362–366.

Murthy, P., Malathesh, B.C., Kumar, C.N., & Math, S.B. (2016). Mental health and the law: An overview and need to develop and strengthen the discipline of forensic psychiatry in India. Indian journal of psychiatry, 58(Suppl 2), S181–S186. doi:10.4103/0019-5545.196828

Mutalik, Narayan & Tp, Tejaswi & Kashinakunti, Manjula & Choudhari, Sb. (2017). Attitude of medical undergraduate and postgraduate students towards psychiatry: a cross-sectional study. Open Journal of Psychiatry & Allied Sciences. 9. 10.5958/2394-2061.2018.00001.0.

Mutheneni, Srinivasa Rao & Morse, Andrew & Caminade, Cyril & Murty Upadhyayula, Suryanaryana. (2017). Dengue burden in India: Recent trends and importance of climatic parameters. Emerging Microbes and Infections. 6. 10.1038/emi.2017.57.

Myers, D.G. (2005). Social Psychology (8th ed.). New Delhi: Tata McGraw Hill Pub. Co. Ltd.

NACO Annual Report, 2016-17

National TB Statistics India (www.tbfacts.org/tb-statistics-india)

Nemade, R., Reiss, N.S., & Dombeck, M. (n.d.). Psychology of Depression- Behavioral Theories. Retrieved March 31, 2019, from https://www.mentalhelp.net/articles/psychology-of-depression-behavioral-theories/

NewIndianXpress. (2018, March 22). 700 Central Armed Police Forces personnel committed suicide in last six years: Union Home Ministry. Retrieved from http://www.newindianexpress.com/nation/2018/mar/22/700-central-armed-police-forces-personnel-committed-suicide-in-last-six-years-union-home-ministry-1790997.html

NewIndianXpress. (2018, September 13). Youth attempts suicide over unemployment. Retrieved from http://www.newindianexpress.com/cities/vijayawada/2018/sep/13/youth-attempts-suicide-over-unemployment-1871313.html

Nicola, Serroni & M. Malouff, John & Thorsteinsson, Einar & Bhullar, Navjot & Rooke, Sally. (2007). A meta-analytic investigation of the relationship between emotional intelligence and health. Personality and Individual Differences. 42. 921-933. 10.1016/j.paid.2006.09.003.

Nizamie, S.H., & Goyal, N. (2010). History of psychiatry in India. Indian journal of psychiatry, 52(Suppl 1), S7–S12. doi:10.4103/0019-5545.69195

O' Donoghue, E.G. (2014). The story of Bethlehem Hospital from its foundation in 1247. Whitefish, MT: Kessinger Publishing.

Oliver, J. (2006). The Myth of Thomas Szasz. Retrieved from https://www.thenewatlantis.com/publications/the-myth-of-thomas-szasz

O'Neill, B. (2017, April 20). You are not mentally ill. Retrieved from https://medium.com/@burntoakboy/you-are-not-mentally-ill-126eb643c347

Pagliery, J., & Griffin, D. (2018, August 28). Jacksonville shooter had history of mental illness. Retrieved from https://edition.cnn.com/2018/08/28/us/jacksonville-madden-shooter-katz-mental-health-invs/index.html

Parikh, S. (2019, February 03). Getting mental health into the curriculum. Retrieved from https://www.thehindu.com/sci-tech/health/getting-mental-health-into-the-curriculum/article26163579.ece

Parry M. (2010). From a patient's perspective: Clifford Whittingham Beers' work to reform mental health services. American journal of public health, 100(12), 2356–2357. doi:10.2105/AJPH.2010.191411

Pennock, S.F. (2015, June 27). Critiques and Criticisms of Positive Psychology @ WCPP2015. Retrieved from https://positivepsychologyprogram.com/critiques-criticisms-positive-psychology/

Per Capita People Living With HIV/AIDS by Country (https://www.nationmaster.com/country-info/stats/Health/HIV-AIDS/People-living-with-HIV-AIDS/Per-capita#-amount)

"Philippe Pinel." Famous Scientists. famousscientists.org. 20 Jun. 2016. Web.3/31/2019 <www.famousscientists.org/philippe-pinel/>.

Powell, E. (2018, October 10). 'Tone deaf' Piers Morgan scolded over calls for mental health overhaul. Retrieved from https://www.standard.co.uk/showbiz/celebrity-news/world-mental-health-day-tone-deaf-piers-morgan-sparks-backlash-over-calls-to-scrap-phrase-mental-a3958416.html

Prentice, R. (2018, March 16). Why We Need to Stop Romanticizing Mental Illness. Retrieved from https://themighty.com/2018/03/stop-romanticizing-mental-illness/

Prest, T. (2009, September 22). Father Joan-Gilabert Jofré and Nuestra Señora de los locos e inocentes. Retrieved from http://idlespeculations-terryprest.blogspot.com/2009/09/father-joan-gilabert-jofre-and-nuestra.html

PTI (2018, August 20). Now avail medical insurance for treatment of mental illness - ET Health World. Retrieved from https://health.economictimes.indiatimes.com/news/policy/now-avail-medical-insurance-for-treatment-of-mental-illness/65469757

Queensland Health, The road to recovery - a history of mental health services in Queensland 1859-2009, Queensland Government, 2013, https://www.health.qld.gov.au/__data/assets/pdf_file/0028/444583/qld-mh-history.pdf.

R Lehman, Darrin & Chiu, Chi Yue & Schaller, Mark. (2004). Psychology and Culture. Annual review of psychology. 55. 689-714. 10.1146/annurev.psych.55.090902.141927.

Rangaswamy T. (2012). Twenty-five years of schizophrenia: The Madras longitudinal study. Indian journal of psychiatry, 54(2), 134–137. doi:10.4103/0019-5545.99531

Read, J., Haslam, N., Sayce, L. and Davies, E. (2006), Prejudice and schizophrenia: a review of the 'mental illness is an illness like any other' approach. Acta Psychiatrica Scandinavica, 114: 303-318. doi:10.1111/j.1600-0447.2006.00824.x

Reddy B, Venkata & Gupta, Arti & Lohiya, Ayush & Kharya, Pradip. (2013). Mental Health Issues and Challenges in India: A Review. International Journal of Scientific and Research Publications. 3. 1-3.

Remembering the father of modern psychiatry who unchained mental patients: 8 facts about Philippe Pinel. (2017, April 20). Retrieved from https://www.indiatoday.in/education-today/gk-current-affairs/story/facts-about-philippe-pinel-972467-2017-04-20

Reynolds, K.J., Turner, J.C., Alexander Haslam, S., Ryan, M.K., Bizumic, B. and Subasic, E. (2007), Does personality explain in-group identification and discrimination? Evidence from the minimal group paradigm. British Journal of Social Psychology, 46: 517-539. doi:10.1348/014466606X153080

Ritchie, H., & Roser, M. (2018, April 20). Mental Health - Our World in Data. Retrieved from https://ourworldindata.org/mental-health#prevalence-of-mental-health-and-substance-use-disorders

Rogers, A., & Pilgrim, D. (2005). Perspectives on mental health and illness. In A sociology of mental health and illness(pp. 1-24). Maidenhead: Open University Press.

Roser, M., & Ritchie, H. (2014, November 03). HIV/AIDS. Retrieved from https://ourworldindata.org/hiv-aids

Roser, M., & Ritchie, H. (2015, November 12). Malaria. Retrieved March 31, 2019, from https://ourworldindata.org/malaria#malaria-death-rates

Ross, M. (2018, September 14). Prince William opened up again about his mental health. Will Charles be mad? Retrieved from https://www.mercurynews.com/2018/09/14/prince-william-opened-up-again-about-his-mental-health-will-charles-be-mad/

Rössler W. (2016). The stigma of mental disorders: A millennia-long history of social exclusion and prejudices. EMBO reports, 17(9), 1250–1253. doi:10.15252/embr.201643041

Rüsch, N., Angermeyer, M.C., & Corrigan, P.W. (2005). Mental illness stigma: Concepts, consequences, and initiatives to reduce stigma. European Psychiatry, 20(8), 529-539. doi:10.1016/j.eurpsy.2005.04.004

Saldanha, A. (2018, February 02). Budget 2018: Health, education, sanitation allocation appears to be most in 3 years but it isn't. Retrieved from https://www.firstpost.com/business/budget-2018-health-education-sanitation-allocation-appears-to-be-most-in-3-years-but-it-isnt-4332137.html

Sambandh Health Foundation (https://sambandhhealth.org/Sambandh/index.aspx)

Schemes under National AIDS Control Programme for NGO's. (2014, March 23). Retrieved from https://indiamicrofinance.com/schemes-national-aids-control-programme-ngos.html

Schneider (2012). Applied Social Psychology, Sage.

Schultz, D. P., & Schultz, S. E. (1992). *A history of modern psychology*. Fort Worth: Harcourt Brace Jovanovich College Publishers.

Schütz A, Nizielski S. Emotional Intelligence as a Factor in Mental Health. Chemnitz (DE): Department of Psychology, Chemnitz University of Technology; 2012.

Sen, A. (2005, November 18). Contrary India. Retrieved from https://www.economist.com/news/2005/11/18/contrary-india

Shah, S., & Anand, G. (2013, October 30). India's TB Spending Slower Than Planned. Retrieved from https://blogs.wsj.com/indiarealtime/2013/10/30/indias-tb-spending-slower-than-planned/

Sharma, S. (2015). Occupational stress in the armed forces: An Indian army perspective. IIMB Management Review, 27(3), 185-195. doi:10.1016/j.iimb.2015.06.002

Shields-Zeeman, L., Pathare, S., Walters, B.H., Kapadia-Kundu, N., & Joag, K. (2017). Promoting wellbeing and improving access to mental health care through community champions in rural India: the *Atmiyata* intervention approach. *International journal of mental health systems, 11*, 6. doi:10.1186/s13033-016-0113-3

Silva, R., Albuquerque, S., Muniz, A.V., Filho, P., Ribeiro, S., Pinheiro, P.R., & Albuquerque, V. (2017). Reducing the Schizophrenia Stigma: A New Approach Based on Augmented Reality. Computational intelligence and neuroscience, 2017, 2721846. doi:10.1155/2017/2721846

Slater, J. (2018, July 10). India is no longer home to the largest number of poor people in the world. Nigeria is. Retrieved from https://www.washingtonpost.com/news/worldviews/wp/2018/07/10/india-is-no-longer-home-to-the-largest-number-of-poor-people-in-the-world-nigeria-is/

Sorolla, J. (1887). Father Jofré Protecting a Madman[Painting].

Srivastava, K., Chatterjee, K., & Bhat, P.S. (2016). Mental health awareness: The Indian scenario. Industrial psychiatry journal, 25(2), 131–134. doi:10.4103/ipj.ipj_45_17

Stadlen, A. (2012, October 04). Thomas Szasz obituary. Retrieved from https://www.theguardian.com/society/2012/oct/04/thomas-szasz

Stallwood, K. (n.d.). THE FIVE STAGES OF SOCIAL MOVEMENTS. Retrieved from http://kimstallwood.com/animal-rights-challenge/4-the-five-stages-of-social-movements/

Statistics, Mental Health (https://www.mentalhealth.org.uk/statistics)

Sternberg, R.J. (1977): Intelligence, information processing, and analogical reasoning: The componential analysis of human abilities. Hillsdale, NJ: Erlbaum.

Sternberg, R.J. (1985): Beyond IQ: A triarchic theory of human intelligence. New York: Cambridge University Press.

Sternberg, R.J. (1990): Metaphors of mind: Conceptions of the nature of intelligence. New York: Cambridge University Press.

Sternberg, R.J. (1997): Successful intelligence. New York: Plume.

Sternberg, R.J. (1999): "The theory of successful intelligence." Review of General Psychology, 3, 292-316.

Sternberg, R.J., & Grigorenko, E.L. (2000): Teaching for successful intelligence. Arlington Heights, IL: Skylight.

Sternberg, R.J., Forsythe, G.B., Hedlund, J., Horvath, J., Snook, S., Williams, W.M., Wagner, R.K., & Grigorenko, E.L. (2000): Practical intelligence in everyday life. New York: Cambridge University Press.

Sternberg, R.J (2007).: Wisdom, Intelligence, and Creativity Synthesized. New York: Cambridge University Press

Sternberg, R.J., & Scott Barry Kaufman (Eds.) (2011): The Cambridge Handbook of Intelligence. New York, NY: Cambridge University Press.

Stuart H. (2003). Violence and mental illness: an overview. World psychiatry: official journal of the World Psychiatric Association (WPA), 2(2), 121–124.

Substance Abuse and Mental Health Services Administration, Community Conversations About Mental Health: Information Brief. HHS Publication No. SMA-13-4763. Rockville, MD: Substance Abuse and Mental Health Services Administration, 2013.

Subudhi, Chittaranjan & Biswal, Ramakrishna. (2016). Mental Health Scenario in India after Erwadi Tragedy.

Survey of London, vol.25 *St George the Martyr, Southwark and St Mary Newton*, Ida Darlington ed. 1955, pp 78 (online version at British History Online)

Swartz, M. S., Swanson, J. W., Hiday, V.A., Borum, R., Wagner, H.R., & Burns, B. J. (1998). Violence and severe mental illness:

The effects of substance abuse and nonadherence to medication. *The American Journal of Psychiatry, 155*(2), 226-231.

Tajfel, H. (1970) Experiments in intergroup discrimination. Scientific American, 223, 96-102

Tanwar, S., Rewari, B.B., Rao, C.D., & Seguy, N. (2016). India's HIV programme: successes and challenges. Journal of virus eradication, 2(Suppl 4), 15–19.

Taylor, S.E. (2006). Health psychology, 6th Edition. New Delhi: Tata McGraw Hill

Thara, R., Padmavati, R., Aynkran, J.R., & John, S. (2008). Community mental health in India: A rethink. International journal of mental health systems, 2(1), 11. doi:10.1186/1752-4458-2-11

THE FIVE YEAR FORWARD VIEW FOR MENTAL HEALTH by Mental Health Taskforce, NHS, England (2016)

The History of Bethlem, p.76, quote from Christ's Hospital minute books

The main source used here is the definitive history by Jonathan Andrews, Asa Briggs, Roy Porter, Penny Tucker and Keir Waddington, *The History of Bethlem,* Routledge, London and New York, 1997

The Optimal Mix of Services, Geneva, World Health Organization, 2007.

Thomas Bowen, *An Historical Account of the Rise, Progress and Present State of Bethlem Hospital,* London, 1783 p. 5n, see also Christine Stevenson's article (below) p.256

Thomas Szasz quotes, Psychiatry as a Human Rights Abuse. (2013, July 17). Retrieved from https://www.cchrint.org/about-us/co-founder-dr-thomas-szasz/quotes-on-psychiatry-as-a-human-rights-abuse/

Thomas Szasz, Professor of Psychiatry, Accolades. (2014, June 19). Retrieved from https://www.cchrint.org/about-us/co-founder-dr-thomas-szasz/thomas-szasz-accolades/

Times Now (2019, January 03). Hundreds of mentally challenged patients chained like animals at Uttar Pradesh's Badaun. Retrieved from https://www.timesnownews.com/mirror-now/in-focus/article/uttar-pradesh-up-badaun-mazhar-mentally-challenged-patients-chained-supreme-court-issues-notices/341107

Tiwary, D. (2018, May 14). To contain suicides, BSF plans annual mental health tests. Retrieved from https://indianexpress.com/article/india/to-contain-suicides-bsf-plans-annual-mental-health-tests-5175675/

Trani, Jean-Francois & Parul, Bakshi & Kuhlberg, Jill & Venkataraman, Hemalatha & Mishra, Nagendra & Groce, Nora & Jadhav, Sushrut & Deshpande, Smita. (2015). Mental illness, poverty and stigma in India: A case-control study. BMJ Open. 5. 10.1136/bmjopen-2014-006355.

Trautmann, S., Rehm, J., & Wittchen, H.U. (2016). The economic costs of mental disorders: Do our societies react appropriately to the burden of mental disorders? EMBO reports, 17(9), 1245–1249. doi:10.15252/embr.201642951

Trautmann, S., Rehm, J., & Wittchen, H. U. (2016). The economic costs of mental disorders: Do our societies react appropriately to the burden of mental disorders? EMBO reports, 17(9), 1245–1249. doi:10.15252/embr.201642951

Tversky, Amos & Kahneman, Daniel (1973). Availability: A heuristic for judging frequency and probability. Cognitive Psychology 5 (2):207-232.

University of Bergen. (2013, January 11). On the mental catwalk: As diagnostic thresholds are lowered, being normal ends up being as difficult as being a Supermodel, philosopher contends. *ScienceDaily*. Retrieved March 28, 2019 from www.sciencedaily.com/releases/2013/01/130111092455.htm

Vatel, B. (2012). A Long and Controversial Career: Thomas Szasz, MD. [online] Psychiatric Times. Available at: https://www.psychiatrictimes.com/bipolar-disorder/long-and-controversial-career-thomas-szasz-md [Accessed 31 Mar. 2019].

Verma, R., Mina, S., & Deshpande, S.N. (2013). An analysis of paramilitary referrals to psychiatric services at a tertiary care centre. *Industrial Psychiatry Journal*, *22*(1), 54–59. http://doi.org/10.4103/0972-6748.123622

Williams, L. (2017, September 10). The unspoken link between income and suicide. Retrieved from https://www.news.com.au/lifestyle/health/mind/the-unspoken-link-between-income-occupation-and-suicide/news-story/c3cffb1e268e2457fef8a334979bde36

Winerman, L. (2006, February). The culture-cognition connection. Retrieved from https://www.apa.org/monitor/feb06/connection

Yadavar, S. (2018, November 23). Led by Odisha, India Reduces Malaria Cases By 3 Million. Retrieved from https://www.indiaspend.com/led-by-odisha-india-reduces-malaria-cases-by-3-million/

Yadavar, S. (2018, September 27). TB Cases Fall, But India Not Doing Enough To Stop The Disease: New Report. Retrieved from https://www.indiaspend.com/tb-cases-fall-but-india-not-doing-enough-to-stop-the-disease-new-report/

Yaseen, Z. (2013). Film Review: The Last Interview of Thomas Szasz. [online] Psychiatric Times. Available at: https://www.psychiatrictimes.com/film-and-book-reviews/film-review-last-interview-thomas-szasz/page/0/1 [Accessed 31 Mar. 2019].

Yerramilli SRR S, Bipeta R. (2012) Economics of mental health: Part I - Economic consequences of neglecting mental health - an Indian perspective. AP J Psychol Med; 13(2): 80-6.

Zhou, W., Yu, Y., Yang, M., Chen, L., & Xiao, S. (2018). Policy development and challenges of global mental health: a systematic review of published studies of national-level mental health policies. BMC psychiatry, 18(1), 138. doi:10.1186/s12888-018-1711-1

Zieger, A., Mungee, A., Schomerus, G., Ta, T., Weyers, A., Böge, K., ... Hahn, E. (2017). Attitude toward psychiatrists and psychiatric medication: A survey from five metropolitan cities in India. Indian journal of psychiatry, 59(3), 341–346. doi:10.4103/psychiatry.IndianJPsychiatry_190_17

Zieger, Aron & Mungee, Aditya & Schomerus, Georg & Ta, Thi & Weyers, Aino & Böge, Kerem & Dettling, Michael & Bajbouj, Malek & von Lersner, Ulrike & Angermeyer, MatthiasC & Tandon, Abhinav & Hahn, Eric. (2017). Attitude toward psychiatrists and psychiatric medication: A survey from five metropolitan cities in India. Indian Journal of Psychiatry. 59. 341. 10.4103/psychiatry.IndianJPsychiatry_190_17.

About the Author

Arjun Gupta is a mental health activist. He decided to promote mental health awareness through his blog and YouTube channel after having battled severe clinical depression between 2015 and 2017. Hailing from Hisar in Haryana, he is currently pursuing an undergraduate degree in Applied Psychology from Delhi University. Supported by the love of his family and friends, Arjun continues to work to make the world a better place; a world that is sensitive to those battling their own minds.

www.ingramcontent.com/pod-product-compliance
Lightning Source LLC
Chambersburg PA
CBHW031106250726

48655CB00004B/1598